CAPTIVE TO CHRIST,
OPEN TO THE WORLD

CAPTIVE TO CHRIST, OPEN TO THE WORLD

On Doing Christian Ethics in Public

BRIAN BROCK

Edited by Kenneth Oakes

CASCADE *Books* • Eugene, Oregon

CAPTIVE TO CHRIST, OPEN TO THE WORLD
On Doing Christian Ethics in Public

Copyright © 2014 Brian Brock. All rights reserved. Except for brief quotations in critical publications or reviews, no part of this book may be reproduced in any manner without prior written permission from the publisher. Write: Permissions, Wipf and Stock Publishers, 199 W. 8th Ave., Suite 3, Eugene, OR 97401.

Cascade Books
An Imprint of Wipf and Stock Publishers
199 W. 8th Ave., Suite 3
Eugene, OR 97401

www.wipfandstock.com

ISBN 13: 978-1-62564-018-5

Cataloguing-in-Publication data:

Brock, Brian, 1970-

    Captive to Christ, open to the world : on doing Christian ethics in public / Brian Brock ; edited by Kenneth Oakes.

    xviii + 144 pp. ; 23 cm. Includes bibliographical references.

    ISBN 13: 978-1-62564-018-5

    1. Christian ethics. 2. Technology—Religious aspects—Christianity. 3. Higher education. I. Title.

BJ59 .B77 2014

Manufactured in the U.S.A.

For Russ
because he asked

Contents

Introduction

Kenneth Oakes

THIS BOOK IS A COLLECTION of edited interviews that took place on various occasions between Brian Brock and several different interviewers. Though the interview can seem lightweight when placed alongside the peer-reviewed article, the research monograph, or the book chapter, it has unique advantages over other genres: the explicit presence of several voices critically interacting; the unexpected twists in argument, flow, and topic; and the immediacy it allows into the speakers' personalities and thought processes. While such generalities are true, and also true of the following chapters, they don't yet express why I find *these* interviews so worthy of consideration.

While studying theology at the University of Aberdeen, I came to know Brian primarily through conversations in departmental seminars, breakfasts after morning prayer, and late nights at St. Machar or the Bobbin. As a completely partial observer, then, what I like most about these interviews are the reminders they offer me of Brian's ability to push one to think harder, to think creatively, and above all to think concretely. Editing this volume also gives me an opportunity to make good on Brian's having introduced me to my favorite question in contemporary jurisprudence: who, exactly, owns the moon?

In order to unpack and anticipate some of the ideas found within the interviews, we could do worse than spend time with one of Brian's heroes: Martin Luther. In his 1531 "Small Catechism," Luther explains the first article of the Apostles' Creed, "I believe in God the Creator," in this way:

> I believe God has created me together with all that exists. God has given me and still preserves my body and soul; eyes, ears, and all limbs and senses; reason and all mental faculties. In addition, God daily and abundantly provides shoes and clothing, food and drink, house and farm, spouse and children, fields, livestock and all property—along with all necessities and nourishment for this body and life.[1]

Notice that for Luther confessing that "God is Creator" entails discussing everyday things like houses, fields, animals, and ears. We are not offered cosmological observations or metaphysical descriptions of God's attributes, but instead a list of things one can find around the house. Notice also that Luther's list includes examples pulled from nature (body, eyes, limbs, children), but also examples from the world of culture and production (shoes, clothing, fields). We could even go so far to say that the examples from culture are also examples of technology, for each requires certain tools, shared and taught practices, and resources dedicated to producing them. Finally, notice also how this explanation of a creedal confession seems on the verge of bursting into praise and thanksgiving for all of the mundane gifts of God. Indeed, how could one confess and understand that God is Creator without experiencing the temptation of offering up praise?

We can find a similar type of reasoning in Luther's "Large Catechism" when he develops the meaning of "give us our daily bread" from the Lord's Prayer:

> God wishes to show us how he cares for us in all our needs and faithfully provides for our daily sustenance. Although he gives and proves these blessings bountifully, even to the godless and rogues, yet he wishes us to ask for them so that we may realize that we have received them from his hand and may recognize in them his fatherly goodness towards us. When he withdraws his hand, nothing can prosper or last for any length of time, as indeed we see and experience every day. How much trouble there is in the world simply on account of false coinage, yes, on account of daily exploitation and usury in public business, commerce, and labor on the part of those who wantonly oppress the poor and deprive them of their daily bread![2]

---

1 Luther, "Small Catechism," 354.
2 Luther, "Large Catechism," 451–52.

Notice again how quickly Luther moves from the prayer Jesus taught his disciples to pray, to God's continual providing for his creatures, and finally to matters of finance, labor, and commerce.

Although they differ in content, both quotations share a common trajectory and ease. As for their common movement, each begins with questions fit for Sunday school and next leaps into talk of food production and distribution, the economic reverberations and motivations for counterfeit currency, the evils of exorbitant interest rates, and the exploitation of workers. In each Luther is pushed into the world of economics in the course of answering ostensibly theological questions about the Apostles' Creed and the Lord's Prayer. He even identifies "God's withdrawing his hand" with a rise in these unjust economic practices. Grace, here, is not divorced from material, economic matters, and Luther in fact views the whole realm of activity dedicated to providing for one's household, or *oeconomia*, with one of the primary ways in which God provides for and blesses his creatures. While the trajectory of the quotations may seem counter-intuitive at first, we could readily substitute the biblical passage or creedal material under consideration and imagine exploring how this would reveal aspects of our own contexts. How might this Luther explain what "release to the captives" means in an age when mass incarceration has become an out-sourced, for-profit business activity? How might this Luther interpret the commandment and promise of Sabbath rest in an age of labor compounds like Foxconn?

As for their ease of movement, each quotation smoothly shifts between the vastly different realms of theology, ethics, pastoral care, and everyday matters. Luther seems blissfully unaware of our sharp divisions between Christian confessions and the material world, or between theology, ethics, and exegesis. Part of this ease is due to the fact that these quotations come from catechetical materials, and that pastors and bishops are often forced to unite what theologians and ethicists are trained to separate. It would not be difficult to find comparable passages in Augustine's *City of God* or Athanasius' *On the Incarnation* that run roughshod over our customary disciplinary boundaries. Here again I think it is no accident that these two bishops/theologians from the past saw little to no difference between theology, biblical exegesis, and dealing with everyday pastoral matters.

There is, of course, no possibility of merely returning to the fourth or sixteenth century. One consolation of the Lord's setting an angel with a flaming sword at the entrance of the Garden from which Adam and Eve had been evicted is that this same angel bars Christians from yearning for a past Golden Age to which we could hope to return. For Christianity, then, nostalgia for past times, with their alleged simplicity and purity, involves looking in the wrong direction. These are the times and habitations appointed to us and so these are the fields in which we must sow, toil, and reap. This still doesn't mean, however, that Augustine, Athanasius, or Luther, in their very ignorance of our disciplinary divisions, can't help illuminate the intellectual habits, fears, and prides of our own age.

Lamenting the present divisions of theology and ethics, Scripture and ethics, or theology and the political is a common enough gesture amongst contemporary theologians. While the typical response to these divisions is to offer a "theory" or "method" for relating disparate fields of inquiry, I take it that Brian's response is actually to perform the overcoming of these disciplinary divides, and to do so in various ways. One of the ways is to look at past theologians and notice how they regularly transgress our divides between doxology, theology, ethics, and exegesis (as we have attempted above). Yet another potential way of circumventing these divides and creating new trajectories of inquiry is by reconfiguring our questions and presuppositions (as we will attempt below).

What happens in theology and ethics, for instance, when Scripture is understood not as a convenient catalogue of interesting facts about God, but as a disclosure of the very world around me and my place within this world? What if Scripture provides not a suspect and politicized historical record of the inner turmoil of an Ancient Near Eastern religion, but is the address and invitation of God? A common temptation when discussing Scripture is to assume that revelation is solely about God, all the while assuming that the world, those around me, and my very own self are simply self-evident. But what I understand Brian to be asking us to consider is that part and parcel of receiving Scripture as revelation is to become alert to how it opens up to us the world as creation and myself as one creature alongside and within this host of other creatures created and loved by God. Seen in this light, Scripture all of a sudden becomes an unruly mixtape of songs, poems, laments, and stories within the history between God and God's creatures.

We might also see the church as the community for whom Scripture is such a disclosure of God, the world, and ourselves. It can be the revelation of God and creation inasmuch as the same God who wrestled with Jacob and Paul still wrestles with us today. Through its promises, commands, and histories Scripture is the address of God to his people and through its stories of praise, of grief, of losing and finding, it teaches us how to address God in return. Stated somewhat more abstractly, we might say that thinking about Scripture and the church, and their interrelationship, best takes place within a wider account of God's dealings with his creatures. Such a lesson can be learned from Barth, or from Luther and his account of the church, the *ecclesia*, as one form of God's care for his creatures.

Within these interviews Brian interacts some with one of the richer contemporary accounts of Scripture, exegesis, and the church offered by the so-called "communitarians." The "communitarians," to use the standard and yet clumsy label, names that group of thinkers who not only think that communities and churches are important (which they are), but who also insist upon a premier place for the church in Christian understandings of theology, exegesis, and ethics. In terms of method and procedure, we might say that communitarians are those who assume that ecclesiology or sociology must act as a kind of "first philosophy," as an intellectual foundation upon which all else is built. Under this category we could include such strange bedfellows as Friedrich Schleiermacher, Stanley Hauerwas, and Leonardo Boff, all of whom are thinkers and people I deeply admire (and with Brian we might get two out of three). Yet one of the persistent tendencies of beginning with the church is that the church also ends up occupying the middle and the end. This is a polemical way of stating the matter, but I think it's illuminating of a certain tendency as well. The response is not that the church is unimportant or unnecessary, but to emphasize how God uses Scripture precisely to bring the church out of itself and into the world, to instruct the church to look elsewhere than itself for its hopes, worries, and guidance. While this vision of Scripture and the church is offered as a kind of indirect criticism of the communitarians, it is not offered in the spirit of any deep antagonism, but as a kind of friendly "pushing," like asking a running partner to do "just one more lap."

We could also imagine what happens when discussions of providence do not directly fasten upon how we should relate different orders of causes or upon how one might respond to genuinely pastoral concerns about evil, suffering, and the efficacy of prayer. Theology and ethics will eventually have to address such concerns, but we could, for a moment, take a cue from Luther and envision God's sustaining of creation within all the natural and cultural processes upon which we as individuals and as communities are dependent. So instead of speaking of primary and secondary causes or radical evil, we might try to speak of God's providence within the contemporary world of monoculture, genetically modified food, and reproductive technology.

This trajectory and ease of movement between matters of Christian doctrine and matters of human interaction and technology hopefully seem less strange by now. For once we begin to name and praise the specifics of God's care for his creatures—food, clothing, water, shelter—we are, just like Luther, led into the realm of material artifacts and thus of technology. It is no exaggeration to say that human life, ever since the first Oldowan stone tool kits, has always been intertwined with technology in the form of learned crafts, the manufacturing of tools and weapons, the organization of the natural world, and the utilization of nature's recurring processes. Human existence and technology are in fact so deeply intertwined that when we ask what it is that preserves, sustains, and saves human life, it seems that technology is more than ready to fill that role. No less than the gospel, then, technology offers its own promises. While technology can certainly modify, recombine, and harness what it finds in ever more dizzying ways, it cannot create in any profound sense of the word.

These remarks are primarily intended to show the deep and natural affinity between doctrines of providence and discussions of technology, and are not meant as any type of blanket criticism of it. Many of us have loved ones whose very existence is predicated upon medical technology, and all of us depend upon technologies of agriculture and water purification. There are, then, no simple or obvious answers to the questions surrounding technology. But theology can offer the world insights into how technology views and forms us as creatures, and how quickly it can assume the mantle of creator and redeemer.

Just as God is present and at work in the mundane matters of providing food for his creatures and hope and consolation for his people, we might also wonder what happens when we view God as present and at work in the messy affairs of human interaction and life together. Jesus does not send his disciples out into a godforsaken wasteland, but out and into his own world, the world of his Father and Spirit. Just as we depend upon agriculture for our daily bread, on the church for learning how to sing praises to God, so too do we depend on a myriad of institutions, organizations, and structures for the goods of peace, safety, and sustenance. Here too, within the realm of life together, God is at work preserving and blessing his creatures, even "the godless and the rogues."

These are hard words to speak and hear, for it is precisely the institutions that shape our life together that seem most corrupt, liable to abuse, and impervious to our hopes and pleas (and perhaps similar words about economics and the church are just as hard). Instead of siding with Luther and his account of politics, or *politia*, as yet another aspect of God's care for his creatures, we might side with the Luther, or with the priest turned heretic in Cormac McCarthy's *The Crossing*, who says that the history of the world, with all its violent struggle, *Realpolitik*, and perpetual subjection of the weak by the powerful, is actually the visible manifestation of God's wrath against sin. Perhaps, then, these are words that can be said and heard only in faith, and like Luther grab the bull by both horns. How, then, can Christians think of mission and political witness within a world that we know belongs to God and yet seems so controlled by the demonic?

Such a context makes all the more provocative Brian's turn to the world of gardening to grasp this dynamic. Within this image the Great Commission sends disciples out into God's garden, his vineyard. Within this garden we do not create the soil, the water, the sun, or the seeds. We till the soil, plant the seeds at the right time and depth, ensure that the level of sunlight and water is appropriate for the plants, and patiently wait on a myriad of forces beyond our control. This is a seductive vision of Christian witness in the world, but once again we might think that the world of politics hardly seems like a garden, and our politicians, interest groups, and violent neighbors hardly seem like roses, daffodils, and tulips. But they do depend on basic aspects of human communication, like trust, that cannot be "made," and that can be courted and encouraged, but are rarely the focus of our discussions of politics and political ethics. The metaphor risks descending into ideology if it is mistaken for an alluring picture of what is a harsh and dark reality.

Despite such justified reservations, I still prefer this account of mission and politics to the other stock-in-trade images of "culture-shapers," "Christian leaders," or even "Jesus radicals" (all rosy-eyed and ideological in their own ways). The power of the metaphor is its ability to admit that God is always and already at work; to show how being receptive and patient isn't the same as being passive and inert; and its sense that Christians should nurture life and growth wherever it is found. Christians can encourage these common and personal goods, and so attempt to be good and honest neighbors, by using their own questions, commitments, and practices. What I find refreshing about the discussion within these interviews is the thought that the goods to which Christians witness could potentially be perceived as beneficial and valuable to everyone, even on their own terms.

We have already invoked two of Brian's theological influences, Luther and Augustine, but the reader should note that these are not your parents' Luther and Augustine. Traditionally, many theologians and ethicists looked to Luther's doctrine of the "two kingdoms," the split between the spiritual and the secular realms, as the most promising of Luther's potential contributions to contemporary thought. By contrast, what Brian finds helpful is Luther's account of God and humanity in his late *Genesis Lectures*, as well as the fluidity and sweeping nature of his account of the "three estates"—economy, the church, and the political—as different forms of God's care for his creatures. As for Augustine, Brian does not focus on the customary resource of Augustine's gritty and rather weary "realism" regarding the ability to enact changes in the social realm, but instead turns to Augustine the exegete, and in particular the exegete of the Psalms. The two other main theological influences, Bonhoeffer and Barth, are once again somewhat different. Brian draws less on Bonhoeffer as a prophet of secularization, and more on Bonhoeffer as interpreter of the Psalms and Genesis. Likewise, the Barth that appears is less the dialectical and neo-orthodox doctrinalist, and more the Barth of the *Ethics* and *The Christian Life*.

In addition to these theologians, a company of various philosophers step onto the stage as well. Thinkers such as Martin Heidegger, Michel Foucault, Friedrich Nietzsche, and Michel Serres all make an appearance, and here again Brian's interactions with their thought (and others) differ from some customary readings of these figures. These philosophers do not serve as occasions for apologetics or spiritual triumphalism in which we can demonstrate the superiority of Christianity. They also do not serve as authorities who must be obeyed. Nor do they become amusing distractions from doing theology and ethics. Rather the sensibility at work here is that nature, history, and culture are vast and complex realities in constant motion, and that those who help to illuminate and uncover these realities are worthy of our attention.

Some final words about the chapters themselves are in order. The first two chapters present an exchange between Brian and two academics working in the university (Herman Paul and Bart Wallet) and thus the densest of the collection. Chapter 1 explores some of the issues raised above regarding the relationship between theology, ethics, and exegesis (focusing on Brian's book *Singing the Ethos of God*), while chapter 2 focuses on how Christians might think about, and at times resist, technology (dealing here with Brian's *Christian Ethics in a Technological Age*). Chapters 3 through 8 each begins with a set question, and the topics under discussion shift as the exchange unfolds. These later exchanges with graduate student Jacqueline Lee Hall Broen are more conversational in tone, and make regular reference to local issues (in Aberdeen and St. Andrews, Scotland) that, when necessary, are given some context in the footnotes. In particular, chapter 3 deals with issues of environmentalism and teaching theology within a public university within a modern nation-state. Chapter 4 opens with a discussion of the politics and problems surrounding energy production and use, then goes into hyper-mobility (the main reason for this production and use), and ends by talking about economy, once again understood as how we provide for and sustain human life. Chapter 5 takes up different forms of Christian community, and shades into a discussion of good works and the dangers of self-promotion, and ends by considering how listening to and caring for others can claim and remake us in unpredictable ways. Chapter 6 begins with Christian higher education, shifts into how such an education could impact local urban planning, and finishes with a discussion of how we might understand heaven, hell, and the end times today. Chapter 7 discusses ways medicine and agriculture are dependent upon forces beyond our control, an observation that opens up to questions of political control, consensus-building, and violence. Chapter 8 handles the place of theology within the university, the use of paranoia within politics and theology, and the importance of being attentive to reality. Many of the chapters are self-contained units, so readers are encouraged to enter the book by beginning with the chapters that most interest them.

The issues covered in the various chapters are certainly diverse. Part of their coherence is found in the recurrence of a set of questions, intellectual moves, and theological themes that are woven into the different parts of the conversations. Their greater coherence, however, is that each seeks to express the polarity given in the title of this work: *Captive to Christ, Open to the World*. At a more general level, the couplet of (1) being captive or bound, with (2) being open or free, challenges the usual idea of freedom as freedom from obligation, influence, and necessity. Ever since Hegel there have been a host of philosophies and ethics that have interrogated this contrast. These accounts have shown how the very real situations in which freedom and constraint are opposed can easily mislead us into thinking that all our duties, relationships, histories, and limitations are just so many burdens and obstacles that prevent us from being truly free, rather than the presuppositions and fields of our freedom.

That being said, the emphasis in the interviews lies in depicting how being captivated by Christ is to be opened to the world. Here the precedents stretch far back: to Luther, Augustine, and Paul. The uniting theme of the interviews is that being captive to Jesus Christ, bound to Scripture, and placed within the church means being made free to receive the world inasmuch as we are placed outside of ourselves, our fantasies and interests, and our communal enclaves. There should, then, be a similar movement in our talk of God in Christ in the world (theology), of Scripture (exegesis), and the worship and practices of the church (ethics). Within the language of theology, we might see this as a riff on Christ's "sending" of his people, with the added improvisation that there is also a "calling forth," inasmuch as Christ meets us in his world, and a "dragging," inasmuch as sin names both the activities and inertia that we use to avoid the complexities and messiness of being a creature in God's good creation. Or we might say that our justification, Christ grabbing us away from ourselves, is the premise of our sanctification, being opened up, emplaced, and given the desire to perceive and receive more of what is already present to us. This captivity means discovering the place we already inhabit and the doors in it that lead outward into other places and other creaturely lives. So we are captured by God as God opens us up to his own presence in and under creatures—which crucifies and resurrects our self-referential and so idolatrous designs on other creatures.

1

Scripture, Modernity, Doxology

Could you please introduce yourself and tell us how you have developed your interest in theology and, more specifically, in the sort of doxological exegesis that your book, *Singing the Ethos of God*, so passionately advocates?

I grew up in a little Bible church in an industrial backwater in Texas. It was a very anti-intellectual world, but one in which the Bible was taken seriously. There was a real sense that faith mattered to life and the Bible was living, rich, and worth reading. So I was taught the content of the Bible, and I was shown that it mattered. This is not to suggest that this upbringing was free of all the problems we might expect from fundamentalist-Puritan-Bible belt southern religion. I can remember smugly chuckling away as my pastor said from the pulpit that education didn't make you wiser, and that PhD just meant "piled higher and deeper." (He didn't mean paperwork, though it would have been a much more insightful comment if he had.) This ecclesial home shaped my understanding of the world, situated as it was in the middle of a pretty bleak landscape of refineries and mind-numbing popular culture. In some vague way I felt stifled and oppressed by the narrowness both of the ecclesial world and the local culture, which is why Scripture represented an outcropping of something ancient and majestic and true that always seemed quite a bit richer than the sermons I was hearing out of it.

This makes it all the more ironic that it was in the midst of the most exhilarating intellectual time of my life that I found that, in a sense, my childhood pastor was right about the tendency of education to cut us off from Scripture. My sense that *Singing the Ethos of God* needed to be written crystallized in an Oxford seminar on the use of the Bible in Christian ethics. In that seminar several world-class biblical scholars and moral theologians gathered in a room full of the English-speaking world's future pastors and academic theologians (and one sitting bishop) to try to discern the ethical implications of a few classic biblical passages. The results were disastrous. Occasional flashes of insight emerged, but we were all left with the overwhelming impression that so much complicated critical machinery had been interposed between us and Scripture that we (meaning primarily academically trained theologians) no longer had the skills to handle it directly. I was shocked and unsettled that the church of the Reformation, the very church that had come into being with the rediscovery of the Bible, could be in such a state. Adding insult to injury, when I went to biblical commentaries to see if they had anything to bring to the discussion of contemporary ethical questions, I found precious little that connected with the burning questions of the age. The conclusion seemed inevitable: the way the theological academy teaches us to conceive our relationship to Scripture makes it difficult, if not impossible, to find our way from Scripture to the ethical questions of our real, lived lives, and conversely, we are taught that the people who are quite obviously doing this (like the Bible-believers I grew up with) were not doing so in an academically respectable manner.

This set me thinking, and more importantly, reading. I discovered that the great theologians of the past not only could and did read Scripture directly and theologically, but their thinking about contentious moral questions often took the form of biblical commentary. They were able to do this because they so regularly practiced the art of theological commentary. Thomas Aquinas, for instance, when he was teaching his students in lecture halls, lectured almost exclusively in the form of biblical commentary. Calvin lectured or preached on Scripture at least one hour every single day. Because modern Christians know these theologians only through their systematic works, the *Summa Theologica* and *Institutes* respectively, we have lost sight of the vast intellectual effort these scholars poured into direct biblical commentary, and how it formed their theologizing. The same can be said of almost all of the great Western theologians before the modern period. I found this fact and its contemporary eclipse striking.

The more I looked into it, the clearer it became that these great biblical interpreters exposed the poverty of modern Christians, and of modern theology and biblical studies. Modern theologians, by and large, have drawn the conclusion after decades of bad experiences with biblical scholars that they don't know enough of the technical details to comment on Scripture. The favor is returned to biblical scholars by theologians who point out that being an expert on one book of the Bible does not qualify you to speak about the whole, which puts one onto the terrain of systematic theology where the various claims that are made in Scripture are balanced and ordered with the aim of forming a coherent body of recognizable Christian doctrine.

Fifteen years ago not many people had yet spotted how far this stalemate removes us from what has passed as theology for our forebearers in the faith, though many more people are alive to this problem now. I decided that the best way to bring this older tradition back into view, in which theology and biblical exegesis went hand in hand, was simply to show the masters at work. This is why the main section of *Singing the Ethos of God* follows Augustine and then Luther as they comment on and draw out what they take to be the ethical implications of the Psalms. I call this "doxological exegesis" because it is interpreting the text of Scripture in the same attentive way that biblical scholars and sometimes theologians do today (exegesis), but it differs from what we have come to expect because it does so before and to God and so as a mode of praise. The Psalms resist being reduced to mere carriers of information because they are so clearly songs of praise. Rather than turning them into "text" from which we attempt to extract "meanings," I've proposed that we begin the other way around: what happens if we read all of Scripture as if what we were engaged in can be done in the mode of a song of praise to God? Hence my title: *Singing the Ethos of God*.

One of your major complaints in the first part of *Singing* is that Christian ethics and biblical exegesis have grown apart. Although this has happened in manifold ways, one consistent tendency, in the modern West at least, is that ethicists have come to favor categorical imperatives, hermeneutical models, and other forms of "theory" or "method" over a mere "listening" to Scripture. Why has this occurred? Has it all started, as you suggest in the introduction (xv), with a feeling of foreignness or estrangement from the Bible—a distance that theory subsequently had to "bridge"? But isn't such a foreignness something experienced in all ages?

I fear that I can't do justice to this question without introducing some technical distinctions. I'll risk beginning with the bold generalization that what we call modern theology is perhaps best understood if we think of it as one long response to a rising tide of secular reason. Secular reason is that form of human reasoning that has consciously decided to think and live without reference to God. The icon of this cultural transition was the famous declaration of the French scientist Laplace, who explained why his scientific theory did not make reference to God with the famous quip, "I have no need of that hypothesis." When enough people agree that certain spheres of reason can and should proceed as if God does not exist, then something like a public secular reason can emerge. This makes sense even to Christians today. Why should the science of meteorology not proceed as if God is not actively involved in changing the weather? But this new intellectual landscape does create new intellectual problems for Christians, who read in the Bible that God sends the rain and speaks in the thunderbolts, and who regularly encounter in their own theological traditions stories like that of Luther, who experienced a lightning strike as a divine word and claim on his life. The fewer people who can think and talk as if a God who acts in history matters, the more Christian theologians have to think about how they are going to communicate what they find important, and how they are going to explain the relation between the rule of natural causality, which science can describe, and God's own working, which seems not to have been left any room to maneuver.

The early modern deists decided that they would resolve this dilemma by saying that God's rule is *through* the natural laws that he has put in motion, and therefore that God either will not or cannot breach the laws of the natural world, and this settlement allowed an idea of God that did not conflict with what scientific observation could tell us about the mechanisms of the natural world. The upshot was that science was taken to tell us about the world, and religion was taken to give us morality and motivation. In this model Scripture must be distilled down to what it tells us about believing in God and about moral ideals and motivation. I would suggest that, in very broad brush strokes, the deists won the day for the majority of modern Christians, which is why the language of "moral principles" is so dominant in modern ethical talk, both inside and outside of the churches, whether conservative or liberal.

In contrast, in the ancient and medieval contexts it was clear that, in different ways, all moral claims were entailments of metaphysical truth claims, and that these claims were directly embodied in different ethics. The Stoics, for instance, viewed the universe as made up of active and passive substances. If this is the constitution of the universe, they reasoned, then it is clear that the appropriate ethic is one in which the major task is to rise above the buffeting of merely earthly circumstances into the realm of the unchanging substances (which is why we now think of someone who is stoic as being rather cold). The Epicureans were the precursors of our modern view of matter as made up of atoms. Believing that all matter is in motion led them to postulate that, since the highest good of humans is happiness, we need to participate in this cycle of change by living a life of sensuous participation in the world, which is why they later came to be caricatured as being given to excess.

This presupposed linkage of metaphysics and ethics continued to hold in the early Middle Ages, as talk about how Christians are to live well was assumed to be an entailment of the metaphysical reality of Jesus Christ's work in the Incarnation, crucifixion, and resurrection as well as his ongoing rule through the Spirit. Within this overarching agreement among Christians, however, another ancient distinction gained new prominence in the high Middle Ages, between thought conceived as separable from and superior to the questions of daily life, labeled "theoretical reason," and those forms of reasoning available even to the unlearned, or "practical reason." "Practical reason" was understood as pertaining to all the remaining knowledge needed to live in the mutable world, the knowledge of when to reap and sow, how to judge a court case, or how to raise children. "Theoretical reason" was concerned with the very structure of reality, with God, space, time, and being, and this was understood to be the most unchanging sort of knowledge. Participating in theoretical reasoning was not a real option for those who did not have the time to dedicate to study, nor was it relevant for the "practical arts," which were understood to be oriented by knowledge about the passing things of this world: how to tell when a cow is about to give birth, or when it is going to rain.

This division of the "theoretical" and the "practical" is the second important conceptual distinction that marks our present, following the drifting apart of reasoning that makes no reference to faith (secular) and reasoning that takes doctrine and Scripture seriously. Modernity can be understood not only as the age of secular reason, but also as the time in which the gap between theory and practice grew wider before collapsing entirely. Immanuel Kant (1724–1804) formalized this distinction in a way that was to have wide reaching implications for modern ethics when he separated his theory of the premises of ethical duty (now called "meta-ethics") from questions about the contexts within which these duty-rules are worked out (now called "special ethics," or "practical reasoning").[1] Within this new separation of practical life from human theorizing about the world, it becomes possible to conceive of ethics, an account of how we are to live, as *derived* from, or reliant on, what we "know," that is, what we believe. Ethics is the discipline within the realm of theoretical reason that gives us the core moral claims that we are to enact in our lived (read "practical reasoning") lives. Understood in this way, the "problem" of ethics becomes how to hold together what "natural" and "theoretical" reason (human reason unaided by revelation and operating at the level of abstractions) knows with the fine textures and situations of daily life. Whereas for the ancients the question was, "Which account of reality best orients one's day to day living?," the modern question is, "How does what I believe relate to how I live?" To be a modern Christian is to experience a split between what is thought and confessed and what is lived, a split that is embodied in the academy in the estrangement of Christian theology and ethics, and again in the split between theology and Scripture.

From a theological perspective, then, "modernity" names that time in which Christians face the problem of finding an appropriate response to secular morality, as well as the temptation to claim they have a "morality" separable from their doctrinal affirmations about the reality of the work of Jesus Christ. It is also the time in which God has largely been reduced to the provider of moral principles, as Kant explicitly espoused. The story of Christian ethics in the last 150 years is lamentable as it is largely a story of succumbing to the temptation to embrace these distinctions. Thus it is not a great exaggeration to say that the whole configuration of modern theology would need to be rethought in order to get anywhere with the problem of the very evident chasm that lies for us between Scripture and ethics. The reality that modern technology has collapsed the distinction between theoretical and practical reason accentuates the need to go beyond the artificiality of the ethics of modernity.

---

1. This distinction is fundamental to the highly influential concept of the "categorical imperative" developed by Immanuel Kant in *Groundwork to the Metaphysics of Morals*.

On my reading, *Singing* is a very "Bonhoefferian" book, even though you make some critical observations on Bonhoeffer's underdeveloped pneumatology. In fact, I have the impression that many of the conclusions could also be derived from a careful, attentive consideration of Bonhoeffer's *Ethics*. At the very least, those Bonhoeffer fragments known as the *Ethics* also lament the modern separation of ethics and exegesis and try to overcome that separation by reconceptualizing Christian ethics as the art of meditation on how God speaks to our heart in prayerful mediation on Scripture. Would you agree? How important is Bonhoeffer to you, as a source of inspiration and as a model of the kind of exegetical theology you have in mind?

This observation of the precise way Bonhoeffer has influenced my framing questions is very well spotted. Bonhoeffer influences my beginning to explicitly theologize in the pivotal chapter 4 of *Christian Ethics in a Technological Age*. Bonhoeffer is important to me because he opens up in two directions: backward into Luther and forward, or laterally, into Barth. I would understand these two thinkers as Bonhoeffer's most continuous and constructive dialogue partners. This is a conversation that I find very rich and that has formed me in many ways. In terms of my own intellectual journey, knowing Barth well prepared me to appreciate what Bonhoeffer was doing, including what he was doing differently than Barth. This has also allowed me to read Bonhoeffer as an example of what it might mean to be a modern theologian who draws from the vast ocean of Luther's theology, which, I would argue, has been the mainspring for the dominance of German theology, and indeed, philosophy, in the modern era.

For instance, Bonhoeffer's notion of prayerful meditation on Scripture is clearly one of the places where he has genuinely been excited by one of the more profound insights of Luther, as I tried to show in *Singing*. Bonhoeffer's highly theological and methodologically aware account of Christian ethics set out in his *Ethics* was also catalyzed by and is a response to Barth's discussion of Christian ethics in *Church Dogmatics* II/2. Barth later responds in his own ways to Bonheoffer's ethical writings in later volumes of the *Church Dogmatics*. I don't always take Bonhoeffer's side in the extended discussion taking place between these three saints, but I always find his investigations illuminating, not least because of their fragmentary nature and the biographical context in which they were forged.

One of the book's key terms is *ethos*. In Aristotle's rhetoric, ethos is a mode of persuasion, distinguished from both logos and pathos. In your account, ethos is related, but not identical, to such terms as "divine drama" (Balthasar), "divine grammar" (Lindbeck), "character" (Hauerwas), and "habitus."[2] Hans Ulrich, in turn, calls it a "place and space of living."[3] Could you please give some terminological clarification? More specifically, what is the advantage of "ethos" over, for example, "character"?

In *Singing the Ethos of God* I discussed the points of convergence and divergence of the ethos or grammar of Christian action as I am using these terms from the accounts found in George Lindbeck and Telford Work. I subsequently wished I had done much more to make clear that my interest is not so much in Balthasarian "theodrama" but in the dramatics of faith. I'm not interested in highlighting the need for an aesthetic grasp of my whole life, nor even, in every case, the whole context of my own action, as the theodrama tradition tends to suggest. I use "dramatics" to indicate the *pro meity* aspect of the life of faith, the reality that if Christ died "for me" and is *my* savior, then it is not illegitimate to pray for divine rescue. I am a recovering stoic Puritan, prone to understanding God as the one who gives us the principles to live by that will get us through life intact if we can just find the repentance and willpower to enact those principles. (Here we can see how the Kantian ethic of principles and the deist ethic of divine non-intervention can fit very nicely together in modern versions of Christianity.) But Barth, Bonhoeffer, and Luther have taught me that we will never save ourselves through living by good principles: we do, in fact, need a living rescuer and ruler. We simply live differently if we live in trust of a person or trusting that we have a good set of guiding principles.

The life of faith is a bit like driving at night a little faster than your headlights allow. This situation is dramatic, in that anything can happen. That something unexpected will happen is a certainty, but we simply cannot know what it will be or when it will happen. But time rolls on and we never escape living in time that we experience as motion. I consider Luther's *Lectures on Genesis* his "systematic" theology, and in it his main concern is to show how God puts people like Abraham, Isaac, and Jacob into motion by calling them to certain tasks, and it is up to them for long stretches of their life to remain faithful to what they have been called to

2. Brock, *Singing*, 264.
3. Ulrich, "On Finding Our Place," 139.

do. They must live according to the divine claim that has been made on them, which means figuring out what faithfulness to that claim means in their so-called "practical reasoning," and yet knowing all the while that they are reliant on God to make sure that they are not thwarted by events they cannot control. They have to wait for things, they are frustrated by twists in the plot they cannot control, and they have to figure out what to do in all sorts of situations. But it is the divine claim that redirects their motion, and it is their faith to attempt to continue on the trajectory this claim has made on them in their daily life. This is not to suggest that each one's life is now organized into a single unified narrative. There are many layers of narratives in which they live, each of which has its own tensions and releases, and their lives as a whole cannot, therefore, be easily grasped by saying that they are making progress, or that they are passing through stages of life because they know God's promises. They can't even say that they know concretely where their lives are going or when they will end. Thus we can say that the life of faith has, in a certain sense, a static structure—we are constantly passing through the doorway of the "now," sometimes under more or less trepidation or satisfaction. I suspect that if I had taken more time to clarify these points in more detail then some of the links with the Luther chapter especially would have been more apparent.

With the term *ethos*, I am therefore indicating overarching types or forms of action that any individual may or may not be enacting in a given moment, the kind of thing we are indicating, for instance, when we say that someone "swaggers." The term *character* has the distinct disadvantage in contemporary usage of directing moral analysis to ourselves as agents, making it very difficult to separate from the quest for self-possession and so for self-satisfaction. Put simply, to ask what I should do in this particular situation in light of the lordship of Jesus Christ and in expectation of his salvation will bring quite different sorts of considerations into view than asking how what I might do in this situation might make me a better and more virtuous person. Hence the danger of self-satisfaction—on one side in using the other person as an occasion for my moral improvement, and on the other in the concern to craft myself into a person who possesses all the virtues. The language I pick up from Luther of the "art of the forgetting the self" is a way of indicating *how* moral deliberation is to incorporate the "I" who deliberates.

Here Kant, with his categorical imperative to never treat others as means but as ends only, lives off of the capital banked by Luther—the right thing to do cannot be good simply because it will contribute to building my character or making me a better person. The forgetfulness Luther espouses cuts off the temptation to tout any moral progress we may have made and that the language of character implies we should be making. I would not deny that in the life of faith we are made into different people, and I hope for the better, but I don't think Scripture allows us to frame Christian ethics as a matter of moral improvement. If this were the case, Jesus would have certainly spent more time praising the brother who stayed home rather than the love of the Father for the prodigal son. Moral improvement is the result, not the aim of Christian ethics. Did David or Sampson achieve a better character through faith? I think not. Did they display a faithful *habitus*? Sometimes more so and sometimes less so. But they certainly had a dramatic life of faith and were never abandoned by a God who kept intervening in their lives and directing them to intervene in those of others. My use of *ethos* intends to name this dramatic feature of faith as well as the fact that their faith waxed and waned, and with it the appropriateness of their actions. Each in their own way displayed moments, whether short or long, of hearing and responding in faith to the divine claim. In my view, learning to read Scripture well involves learning to identify the points when such biblical characters exemplify a proper ethos of faith and those other points when they are examples of yet another form of self-serving ethos. In this usage "ethos" is therefore naming the observable grammar of the ways they are *enacting* faith—are they "swaggering" or "slouching"?

I'm following Luther here in suggesting that the way we move in life flows from the comportment of the heart, and here the Psalms help us to see the inner dialogue with God that characterizes the faithful moments of the biographies of many biblical characters. David is not the most prominent psalmist by accident: his was an exemplary faith and relationship with God, and his psalms offer all Christians a faith that they can embrace wholesale because they depict the heart's wrestling with God over the dramatics of life. When we look at his biography, it is clear that sometimes David's heart was harder than others and therefore his acts were examples of ways of living we should also avoid.

Using driving to illustrate these points is therefore appropriate because of its modesty in suggesting that when we talk about Christian ethics issues of style are not in the foreground except to the extent that they help us discern our stance toward God. "Blessed are those" says the first verse of the Psalms, "who do not walk in the way of sinners" (actively pursuing with the crowd those things which God detests), nor do they "sit in the seat of scoffers" (stopping and taking up residence with the skeptical and endlessly ironic). Notice that "sitting like a scoffer" brings a certain image to our mind that indicates not only a mode of human investment of energy that is self-destructive, but also one which is made visible by the tonality of the sitting—it displays a comportment of the heart. This is what I mean by "ethos." Driving as an example of faith reminds us that yes, there are rules of the road, but a good driver is not reducible to a good rule follower. Driving can't be done at all without shaped perceptions and reflexes that have a different bodily logic than the rules that the driver must obey, and have to do with momentum, acceleration, and deceleration, a feel for how the controls work, and so on. I want simply to stress that God takes us out of our comfort zone, and that in such places we must live by hope and from the promises of God as given to us in Scripture. This means that we never have the script memorized, but must always go back to Scripture and "chew" on it in the hope that God will remind us of how he has promised to be toward us, and so set our hearts aright.

The second key term is "singing." As I understand you, singing stands opposed to criticism in two significant ways: (a) it praises instead of analyzes, and (b) is a matter of first-order participation rather than second-order observation. I'm sure, however, that our readers need some explanation at this point. So, what is so important about singing? And, in practical terms: what does it imply for our congregations (for our sermons, catechetical practices, hymn singing, and so forth)?

You've clearly hit on my two main terms, and I have to resist saying that the whole book is a response to this question! Your two summary points are spot on, so thank you for so nicely encapsulating two of the book's key emphases.

"Singing" names a human stance that refuses to think of God and humans as entities that are conceivable without reference to the other. I think the creation stories of Genesis open the story of God and humans with a clear reminder that we were not meant to be autonomous. We are not happier or healthier when we go it on our own without God. It therefore questions the very heart of modern, Western ethical culture, which is based on the idea that we are meant to become morally self-aware and self-responsible beings, that is, autonomous. Whatever else we might say about the Fall, we probably ought to say that because we are fallen we find it exceedingly difficult to think of God and humans in right and continual relationship.

I'm interested in what happens when we stop thinking of God as a deist God who has provided us, through Scripture, with the "moral principles" we need to live a good life and then stepped out of the picture. If this is the way things really are then anyone who picks up the instruction manual can work out the rules of the game. This is the insight of the communitarian account of Christian ethics, which refuses to think of Christian ethics as a matter of principles that can be learned by an individual, but insists that Scripture is tied to a community. But the communitarians don't make a second move that I think is important, which is to ask how God is present to us, and how this presence ought to shape our action in every sphere.

This second move is crucial. When we ask "what is God doing?" the first thing that happens is that, if we take Scripture seriously, we start to see that God is at work and present to us in an infinite number of ways. God has provided the means of our daily sustenance and ensures that the fertility of the plant and animal world does not dry up and so starve us. The continuance of the human race as a whole depends on a similar type of divinely gifted fecundity. The sources of this fecundity cannot be controlled, though we do try. In addition, we cannot bring about peace between people, neither in our homes nor in our societies as a whole. We can court and invite peace between people, but we cannot *create* it. None of these things can be unilaterally forced, but must be invited, awaited, received. When we try to manipulate things like political consensus with spin doctors or governments by opinion polls, we do not live as if it is God who must bring peace between people but take it upon ourselves to ensure that peace, like everything else, is a product we can produce if enough effort and skill are applied, like the sausage we can count on appearing if we fill the machine at the top and turn the crank. We aim to do the same with the fertility of the natural world and human fertility. We would be much more comfortable if we could get it all under control, running smoothly to our schedules. Or at least this is the aspiration I call technological. Thus "singing" and "technology" are the opposing poles that shape contemporary Christian faith, and my two books can be read as exploring the one question of the appropriate ethos of the Christian but beginning from different ends of this spectrum. The term "ethos" allows me to say that in some points and in some ways I am living as if Christ is Lord, and in other parts of life (perhaps unbeknownst to me) I am trying to get my way and rule my personal world, if not the whole world.

You have written, "What we trust we praise; the form of our faith is detectible in our praises."[4] I think this is an important insight, especially for those of us infected by the "hermeneutics of suspicion" underlying so much of our (academic) criticism. More specifically, one might conceive of criticism not only as an anti-doxological activity, but also as an implicit form of self-praise. At the very least, our criticism tends to presuppose our own ability to judge, and also often our superiority over those whom we subject to criticism. This made me wonder whether, perhaps, the real difference between praise and criticism is the position of the subject. Isn't praise an "art of forgetting the self"? (Think of how Bonhoeffer, following Luther, describes the Christian life as the process of being liberated from the *cor corvum in se* [the heart that is turned in on itself].)

You have nicely captured my interest in using doxological language in order to expose our tendency to praise our various quests to go it alone and to save ourselves in what we think is a less incriminating key. I take this to be a contemporary restatement of the priority of grace that the Reformers recovered from the church fathers and Scripture.

If the appropriate and truly human stance before God is one of praise, and therefore of service and witness, it is deeply problematic to pursue any type of project in which self-conscious attempts to shape our lives become a primary objective rather than an effect of having been claimed by others in ways that inevitably give our lives a shape. This is the problem of the *Lebensphilosophie*-type approach that has gained so much ground in German practical theology, and of the English-speaking offshoots of liberal and post-liberal theologies that understand Christian ethics as churchly deliberation about the formation of "our" identities. In these intellectual traditions the church is understood to be drawing on a stock of traditional and biblical images to make collective decisions about who it will be. It is precisely this quest to form identity, albeit in a Christian way, that drove the early development of the English-speaking communitarian ethics movement, which you rightly note that I criticize.[5]

---

4. Brock, "Attunement to Saints Past and Present," 161.
5. This criticism appears in Brock, *Singing*, ch. 2.

In my view, quite a lot would have to be adjusted if we began to try to disentangle the contemporary English-speaking communitarian discourse from its deep enmeshment in the more common modern search to "define my identity" that so completely dominates the liturgies of our secular-consumerist-Facebook culture. Yes, I think that we become readers of Scripture in the ecclesial community, but if we are to be really incisive interpreters of our present, we need to be able to see the ways in which our contemporary ecclesial communities are in lockstep with the gods of the age. To do this, I suggest in *Singing*, we need to widen our concept of the community with whom we are learning to interpret Scripture to the saints throughout the ages. Saying this puts the discussion of how our "reading community" forms us in a very different conceptual register than it does for those whose primary interest is in how we speak and live in ways that make us fit in with our workmates, our national cultures, and even our local church communities. It is an ecumenical vision in the widest possible sense.

I am glad that you offer such a thoughtful, spiritual alternative to the "modern obsession with method."[6] But isn't there a risk of overstating the contrast between your own position and the methodological discourses you criticize? Let me put the question this way: once prayerful meditation on Scripture is our starting point, how then does "criticism continue to function"[7]? It is difficult to imagine biblical exegesis proceeding in a manner entirely devoid of rules or guidelines, as you seem to suggest elsewhere with your comment that, "Good readings are ones in which multiple traditions meet to reveal new complexities of God's truth."[8]

My question is: where does methodological reflection take place? At what point in the reading of Scripture do we stop and think, "Do I have this right"? I am certainly not denying that we should think hard about this question of "understanding rightly" and in a way that can be rationally explained. The dominant answer to this question is offered by modern criticism, which assumes that we can ask this question *before* we start reading. Phenomenologically speaking, this is a sleight of hand. We are born into and move in and out of traditions that shape our reading, this modern critical

6. Ibid., xiii.
7. Ibid., 311.
8. Ibid., 279.

tradition as well as many others. There are "naïve" pre-critical exegetical traditions easily to be found in Christian churches, especially those Two-Thirds World churches that have so quickly become the majority of world Christianity, not to mention the pre-critical interpretation that formed the backbone of Christian theology. Put bluntly, if we insist dogmatically that the modern form of criticism is the only form of criticism, then we will end up looking down on most of the Christian tradition of exegesis as well as most of the world's Christians who do simply read the Bible without starting out with the methodological discussions that essentially stalled the Oxford seminar on the Bible and ethics I referred to above.

We ask the question of exegetical method, then, in the middle of several impasses. On the one hand we have the "naïve" readers of the contemporary churches around the world, who just get on with reading in all sorts of ways, according to the standards of good reading in their own communities, and we have the scholarly Western church, which has a real problem getting from the Bible to ethics and back. Some take the Bible as Scripture and have no critical relation to it, and some know how to treat the Bible as "text" but not as "Scripture." Neither, it seems to me, offers a working account of how we are to understand the role of past readers of Scripture in shaping our own ways of reading it.

It is indisputable that we can think about *how* we read Scripture, a form of thought that has been called hermeneutics and that raises questions—crucial questions—about the ways we are reading a text in order to make it more rigorous and rationally explicable. This is one of the ways of thinking that marks theologians today as *modern* theologians, and this sensitivity is a gift of the transition from Christendom into our current setting in which secular reason is dominant. But it is also historically observable that any "rules" or "guidelines" we might formulate as we read are ones that are constantly being revised and sharpened in the face of a canon of Scripture that remains fixed. "Rules" and "guidelines" may well be the way a given reading tradition gives us access to Scripture, but they do not ensure critical reading, nor do we learn them and learn what they mean before we begin to read.

Putting the point more practically: I am writing a commentary on 1 Corinthians with Bernd Wannenwetsch. In the course of our attempts to comment on the chapters in the order that they are presented by Paul we occasionally stop and pursue methodological questions, asking what larger theological presuppositions are at stake as we try to interpret this or that passage. We had a long debate about whether or not to open the book with an introduction or a preface. Our having such a debate flows from our shared insistence that any discussion of *method* be tied to the *content* that we are trying to interpret. If we are forced to admit that we have hermeneutical rules, then we have only one: that methodological reflection always be tied to the text being interpreted in the context in which it is being interpreted, that is, in the context of our more temporally and geographically local church as the place from which we interact with the universal church. Methodological reflection is thus ineradicably tied to the communion of saints. To read Scripture is to hear those who wrote it amidst those contemporary Christians with whom we are also talking and in whose language we must speak if we are to read at all. In the deepest sense this means that all theology is biblical translation.

If you are right about the role and place of method among Christian ethicists, it might well be argued that we postmodern churchgoers without any education in theology, often suffer from the opposite problem: we do whatever we think or, more often perhaps, feel is appropriate for a twenty-first-century Christian, even if that runs counter to traditional Christian lifestyle precepts. Sure, we pray before eating our industrially farmed meat, we ask God for help as we start another sixty-hour work week, and sincerely hope that our mortgage will allow us to donate some money to a charity. And, yes, we also read our Bible. We agree that this may raise difficult questions—in our Bible study group, we wonder whether we are still obliged to tithe—but do not seriously consider those ancient moral prescriptions, written for Jews or Christians some thousands of years ago, as binding for us. We would rather quote Romans 14: "Each one should be fully convinced in his own mind."

Granted that there might be some exaggeration in this portrayal, don't you think that, in this specific context, your aversion to method and hermeneutics may have a counter-productive effect? The problem is not an overabundance of method; the problem is that we, in spite of our sinful habits, honestly believe we live a Christian life. And as long as it is commonly accepted that we can justify that claim by appeal to individual experience or conscience, no Bible study group (the communitarian solution) is likely to correct us. Therefore, don't we postmodern Christians need theologians who tell us firmly: understanding yourself as part of the Christian story implies that you live out that story

by giving up your materialism, consumerism, and workaholism? Don't we need theologians who dare to challenge our "Christian behavior" by simply pointing out that there are well-established *rules* for biblical exegesis? Gordon J. Wenham has the same worry: "Individualism can run riot, and all sorts of outrageous ideas may be claimed to be justified on the basis of meditation on the Scriptures."[9]

The best way to answer this question, very much in agreement with your awareness of the tight linkage of reading and living, is to indicate how I think that the rejection of interpretative rules works in practice. In 1 Corinthians 6 Paul discusses the problem of Christians going to prostitutes and then defending their behavior as non-moral on the grounds that what we do with our bodies does not save or damn us. (Notice that both the defenders of this behavior and their opponents would have found it easy to invoke the "be convinced in your own mind" interpretative rule!) Writing from his professorial desk in the small and charming North England town of Durham, in the early 1960s, C. K. Barrett did not feel very close to the Mediterranean culture of the first century. This led him to locate the problem of *porneia*, and so Paul's rather strong injunction to "flee" it, firmly in the past: "Temptations to fornication were so common in Corinth that mere disapproval was likely to be inadequate; strong evasive action would be necessary."[10] Barrett is clearly imagining that the Corinthians "back then" lived in a sex-soaked age that he experienced as distant from his own experience. And in fact this distancing is fundamental to the understanding of biblical criticism that is dominant in biblical studies. We must first ask what the writers of Scripture meant to say in their own contexts, and *only then* can we ask if it has any relevance for us. This distancing of our present from the "past" in which Scripture resides makes perfect sense within the hermeneutical rules of the guild of modern critical biblical studies, which forces us into the position of having to see the Corinthians as in no way our contemporaries. This is what I am referring to when I say modern biblical studies rests on an assumed gap between Christian ethics and Scripture.

But what happens if we try to take Paul a little more seriously as *an apostle*, and the Corinthians as human beings with sexual drives and maybe even a sexualized culture not so unlike our own? The cultural changes in motion since Barrett's day make it a little more difficult to maintain the

---

9. Wenham, "Reflections on Singing the Ethos of God," 119.

10. Barrett, *Corinthians*, 150.

illusion that somehow the Corinthians had a lot of explicit sex in their society whereas, we, for instance, have done away with cultic prostitution. The backdrop of our experiences of the role of sex in advertising, the sexualization of children's fashion, the mainstreaming of pornography, the intertwining of the porn industry with other more reputable industries all make it more difficult to meaningfully preserve the belief that we are culturally distant from the Corinthians. If we are paying attention to developments in our Western cultures then we can already call on a range of first-hand experiences through which we can begin to glimpse ways in which we are closer to the Corinthians of the 50s AD than biblical criticism likes to admit. We read in the papers every day about people's claims that what they have done online should not be held legally liable because it was "just talk" or "just trading pictures" that hasn't harmed anyone. The moral argument here seems quite close to the Corinthian believers who were going to prostitutes and defending it as "none of the church's business." If we take Paul seriously as the *church's* apostle, and not just the *Corinthians'* apostle, then as we read him we may well find ourselves faced by the question of whether we are more like the Corinthians than we had at first assumed. But we will only be able to hear the apostle put this question to us if we do not insulate ourselves with the modern assumption that people in the past were somehow more primitive thinkers or were less morally sophisticated, suffering from problems and malformations of faith that we have somehow surmounted as participants in a later and supposedly more developed era.[11]

The way the gospel in this biblical passage will change us is not because we will discover in it a general rule for all ages, but because as we read it the Spirit convicts the church: "What we are doing on our computers is not right, and we repent and seek new ways of living." Sex is an easy target for this point, but I think the same sort of process is true across the whole of human existence, not only in our sexual practices, but in our practices of work, politics, and even our eating. Those Christians who are pushed out of the comfortable stasis of the habits of their own age and begin repentantly to explore alternative ways of living are the true and powerful witnesses to the gospel's power to change the world because they display precisely how different habits can be discovered in which new life is found. As an ethicist I can prepare the way for this conviction and explorative response by asking about all sorts of modern ways of life: "have you thought about this?" But

11. For more on this theme see Brock, with Wannenwetsch, "Ein moralisches Angebot," 92–97.

I am wary of the Pharisaism of having all the answers for others, which is always seductive to moral theologians.

Earlier in this series we interviewed Richard Hays and asked him how *The Moral Vision of the New Testament* could spend hundreds of pages on what one might call a moral hermeneutics without referring more than in passing to the work of the Holy Spirit in the hearts of those who read the Bible for moral instruction. Although Hays agreed that his pneumatology ought to be further developed, he added that the hermeneutics outlined in *The Moral Vision* does not at all intend to exclude divine inspiration or the indwelling of the Holy Spirit. In fact, he hoped his hermeneutics would offer "a hermeneutical specification of the guidance of the Holy Spirit and the presence of Christ, in the hope that these are more than pious phrases." Obviously, it is easy to criticize this line of thought ("How could you ever pretend to capture the Holy Spirit in a model?"). Yet, at the same time, isn't there some wisdom in Hays's refusal to see "hermeneutics" and "inspiration" as mutually exclusive?

It is often said that the term *hermeneutics* derives from Hermes, the god of communication. Hermes has, at least in contemporary discussions, become synonymous with the messenger angel responsible for carrying messages between distant places. This intermediary can thus reveal how things that seem chaotic and random on their surface are actually expressions of hidden patterns. Hermes is the god who drops ideas into our head that do not follow from the surface reading of things, and so names that moment when we make unexpected connections between things that seem totally unrelated to each other on first glance. I have in mind moments like those in childhood, when we notice that the ripples in the sand in the water at the beach have the same shape and pattern as the cirrostratus clouds above, high in the atmosphere. Hermes has become the placeholder for that the "click," the "aha" when we see how one pattern can be the double of another from a very different place, with the effect that both become much more obvious and intelligible. This ancient Hermes I like very much, he sounds like the work of the Spirit to me, but I experience the modern discourse of hermeneutics as hermetic—largely sealed and dead—and as such an enemy of making such rapid and surprising connections. As a discipline modern hermeneutics seems much more interested in telling me what I cannot say than what I can say. Like all criticism it can only say "no," not teach us how we are going to actually say "yes." This parallels the driving example above, in that the rules of the road tell us what we must not do, but simply ignore the problem of telling us how to get a car moving.

I have just given an example about how we might understand the Spirit to find connections between our lives and that of the worlds of Scripture, the example of 1 Corinthians 6. On my reading the work of the Spirit in relation to Scripture is precisely to make such unexpected connections. When I read the tradition of premodern Christian exegesis, what I see are many such breathtaking leaps being made. But when I read texts in the modern discipline of hermeneutics, including the Christian versions, it looks to me like it wants to justify or judge the surprising leaps of good reading that must happen and that it nevertheless cannot truly explain. Criticism therefore always comes after the fact even though it rhetorically positions itself as taking place before. Hays, for instance, is a good reader of Scripture, not because he has good hermeneutical rules, but because he pays attention to the actual flow of the text in a theologically attuned way, making wonderful theological connections. I would offer him as another example of the way the modern theological hermeneutics in fact must rest on theological and exegetical claims that in most cases are much more interesting than the hermeneutical rules that are supposed to summarize how good biblical interpretations have been produced. Speaking biographically, I decided to write *Singing* in part because I was terribly bored by reading hermeneutic theory, and had tired of hearing people who were good at talking about it, but could never bring any living water from Scripture. I had enough experience of Christians and of traditional exegesis to know that if we are forced into an either-or situation, there is more to be gained from those who know more of Scripture and less of theory than the other way around. So I went looking for Hermes and the Spirit found me.

Hermeneutical rules are not like a machine you can turn on to manufacture interpretations. That we even aspire to such a machine says more about our participation in a rival modern technological tradition than it does about the content depicted in Scripture. The experimental musical compositions of the 1960s and 1970s that consisted in several tape players going slowly out of synchronization, serial composition, or Jackson Pollock's mechanistic automaton paintings showed us what it looks like when we defeat ourselves by trying to do away with Hermes, or the inspiring Spirit. I agree that we should test interpretations by reference to doctrine, but I do not agree that the guidance of the Holy Spirit can be specified with hermeneutical rules, especially not in advance. Moreover, the best Christian exegetes may have a set of interpretative moves on which they regularly rely, but they would never say that they first had their hermeneutic theory right before they interpreted. If push came to shove, this is why I would still posit an antithesis between what the modern hermeneutics discourse asks of Christians and what has characterized the church's own ways of teaching believers to understand Scripture rightly as described in Scripture and as practiced in the majority of the Christian tradition.

A related problem, or a similar sort of question: In a response to your book, Wenham criticizes you for being too critical of the communitarian approach. In his view, the communitarians rightly identify the Christian community (the church) as the *locus* of Christian ethics. In your reply, you merely repeat a point made in *Singing*: that the communitarians, in your reading at least, "are so sure that they are the Church that close reading of Scripture seems to fade in importance."[12] But this, I would say, is two conflate two distinctions: (a) between close reading or not, and (b) between individual and communal practices of reading. I wholeheartedly agree with your insistence on the need for close, attentive reading of God's Word. But the question is: do we practice such reading alone, sitting in our private chamber with the door shut (Matt 6:6), or in the community that God has given us? Is close reading an individual or, as Wenham takes the communitarians to argue, a communal activity? I have the impression you must agree with Wenham at this point, especially if you write that "individual praise is only knowable as it harmonizes with the body of Christ."[13] So, aren't you too critical of the communitarians?

When talking about reading the Bible, modern Protestants almost inevitably find themselves caught within a binary polarization of the individual and the communal. If, then, one raises questions about communitarian readings, the optical illusion is immediately created that individual readings are being championed even if no arguments are being made to that effect. Put bluntly, I think reading *Scripture* as an individual is a conceptual impossibility. Conceptually speaking, to call the Bible "Scripture" is to admit a specific type of relation to a sharply demarcated body of believers. At no point in all the processes of composition, canonization, and

12. Brock, "Attunement to Saints Past and Present," 159.
13. Ibid., 162; see also Brock, *Christian Ethics in a Technological Age*, 247.

preservation and handing on to us did any single person get to say what it "meant." They were always part of a community that preceded them and who had already formulated some very precise statements about who God is. Let me put it this way: how did the evangelist Luke know that it was appropriate to place a song of praise, the Magnificat, on Mary's lips, and a similar song on Simeon's lips? Luke was part of two traditions: the first was one of psalmody, in which he learned what counted as a psalm, and therefore fit perfectly with what he knew of God's working and the person Mary, and the second was one of what biblical scholars call "inset poetry." Luke knew that the songs of Mary and Simeon would stand for us as readers as an invitation to sing their song with them. To write the story this way (and I believe the biblical authors had some liberty to compose those truths God had revealed to them) was an invitation to all the believers in this same God who would read it in the future. Saint Luke could know it would stand as such an invitation because he knew from books like Exodus, Samuel, and Jonah that such songs of praise are regular features of biblical narrative and occur at high points of the narrative at which we are already tempted to praise the mighty works of the Lord.

I have criticized the communitarian account of reading Scripture within the church in a manner that affirms their central interest in the church, but pushes it one step further by showing that perhaps they still do not take the church seriously enough as *God's* people. Namely, there are many "communities" and only one "church," so already to call the church a "community" hints at a fairly important theological danger. The whole force of *Singing* is, first, to show the many ways in which there is a conceptual and theological difference between an "individual" reading a "book" and a "Christian" reading "Scripture," and the main one is that Christians are never reading on their own. Second, it argues that there is no recipe for generating correct readings, including, as you note, any claim that "we gathered Christians have prayerfully talked this over, and so our readings must be correct." The later generations of communitarians have shown much more awareness of this second point than the earlier generations who did not admit it at all.

I simply insist that the Spirit has to open the Bible to us—we cannot force that process by rushing it or manipulating it, including ensuring that we will get it right by reading it in groups—because we cannot escape reading it in groups! It is certainly possible to approach reading Scripture with a wrong understanding of what the Bible is (tied, of course, to a wrong idea about what faith is), a view that may indeed be sub-Christian. We need the Spirit through the Bible to break in on us if, for instance, we think the Bible is a "resource" for *our* "moral identity formation" undertaken in "group discussions of moral questions"—the classic communitarian account of the church and its relation to Scripture that is the target of my criticisms. My main problem with the communitarians is not that they want the church to read Scripture together, but that they are often trapped in descriptions that tend to make this reading an aspect of a process of *self*-formation. This is why I stress that what we need to ask about criticism is how *God* is using Scripture to criticize our thought and practice. I ask this because I think that if Christians are going to have a living witness, it is crucial that they are drawn a little further out of themselves, and to do this means releasing Scripture from its captivity to moral self-formation, however conceived.

As a historian/philosopher of history, I am not entirely sure what to make of the criticism of "the belief in epochs" that Bernd Wannenwetsch deploys when responding to *Singing*.[14] I cannot help thinking that his insistence on the mutual exclusivity of epoch-thinking and tradition ("We can only believe *either* in epochs or in tradition, and those who confess the *communion sanctorum* certainly do the latter") is overstated, and maybe also unfair. For tradition isn't monolithic, is it? Precisely because the saints, just like the rest of us, all have their distinct voices, it would be a great loss if we were not allowed to explain their distinctiveness "on the basis of what we (think we) know of the respective epoch in general." Contextual explanations of, for example, Augustine's biblical exegesis, do not aim to "explain him away," but, to the contrary, to understand in full detail the particularity of what this "member" adds to the "body." Since it seems you tend to agree with Wannenwetsch, I would like to ask your opinion.

The crucial question is: with whom are we contemporaries? I would like to answer "with Christ and *his* people." I say "would like to" because I must admit that I more easily see eye to eye with, say, someone with whom I share a hobby than someone at church. If I were plopped into the tent of Abraham, would he seem like my father in faith, or if we were to be honest, a pretty crazy guy from another age? We'd be sitting in his tent, and if we were joining in his worship of God, we could be certain that he would be

14. Wannenwetsch, "Conversing with the Saints," 130.

carrying out this worship in ways that would feel very odd to us. So are we worshipping the same God? The Letter to the Hebrews tells us that this is our father in the faith. Can we afford not to see eye to eye with him?

I am trying to raise Christians' awareness that on close inspection it may be the case that in fact we do not share the same time with the people next to us in the pew and so are not their contemporaries. Conversely, we may be so completely their contemporaries that we cannot understand the faith of the many generations of our fathers and mothers in the faith. If you read the moral treatises of the church fathers you cannot help but face this question. How do we account for the fact that we can find ourselves resonating so strongly with much of the theologies of an Augustine, Aquinas, or a Luther but have such strikingly different accounts of how to live our lives? This is a problem that is obscured by an "eternal principles" model of Christian ethics, which assumes that some sort of averaging process across all the moral cultures of Israel and Christendom will give us the basic moral rules for Christians today. But once we've gotten these rules, aren't we better than Abraham? Doesn't this commit us to saying to Abraham, "I know you are the father of faith, and that faith is something one lives, but your morals were all messed up." We would be sorely tempted to tell him that it was imprudent for him to send a servant to find Isaac's wife for him, and, while we were at it, we might as well tell Jacob he was pretty irresponsible to marry Leah without getting to know her a little better. This stance of superiority is endemic in modern ethical theory and parallels the sense of self-importance of modern hermeneutical theory. Both mean we end up not being able to make much of most of the stories of faith in the Bible.

Michel Serres provides a helpful example of what I mean by this counter-intuitive understanding of contemporaneity.[15] A late-model car is, of course, a modern object. But we have it only because ideas and practices from previous ages were drawn in and incorporated into the agglomeration we see before us. The wheel was invented in Neolithic times. I am doing something, using a wheeled object, which has been done for millennia, and in doing so I am the contemporary of the earliest humans pushing a cart. I just do it with less effort. Internal combustion was invented in the nineteenth century, and so in driving a car I am the contemporary of Henry Ford and all the owners of the Model T against all other times and places. At the furthest end of the spectrum I am not a contemporary of those who drive Lamborghinis, and I probably never will be. I'll never join a

15. Serres with Bruno LaTour, *Conversations on Science, Culture, and Time*, 45.

Lamborghini owners' club, go on a rally with them, talk their talk or be part of their "crowd"—they live in a world that is inaccessible to me. Yes, we are contemporaries as wheel users, and as internal combustion machine operators, but for them other games have been added, such as the game of race car mimicry and the game of conspicuous consumption in which we must not only buy and be seen with such objects, but must know which objects to buy and be seen with in order to be socially successful. Within one frame of reference the poor kid riding to work on a bicycle and the Lamborghini owner are contemporaries as wheel users, but in real life this contemporaneity is not the one that counts, or it only counts because the Lamborghini club members see this shared use of the wheel as proof of their superiority. Contemporaneities are therefore not about time, but about communities, and the ways in which communities organize perception and define what counts as a good action.

Wannenwetsch's refusal of epoch-thinking, on my reading, parallels Serres' point in being an attempt to break up our habit of separating our age as a whole from all others in preference for a vastly more differentiated view. We are always making gestures that are ancient, early modern, and cutting edge. We are therefore with some people behind the times, with others in our present time, and with a few others doing what everyone else will be doing in a few years. Epoch-*thinking* breaks up this diversified awareness by thinking in terms of large arcs of time in which everyone exists, only to be left behind by the birth of a new epoch. If epoch-thinking has any utility it has to show the ways in which we are *still* parts of epochs that are only apparently over. Why, for instance, does Augustine's *Confessions* still seem so accessible to us today, so modern, at least in its biographical first half? The point of Wannenwetsch's comment is to invite us to begin questioning our modern habit of assuming that everything from the epoch before modernity was more "primitive" than we are, that those Christians were therefore *less* sophisticated than us. To understand ourselves properly as moderns we have to see there are many points of unity between us and people in other ages that this undifferentiated epoch-thinking obscures. Most importantly, if we do not have the faith of Abraham, Isaac, and Jacob, we better not think of ourselves as "church"—because we are grafted onto *that* branch. If we can live the same faith as the psalmists, if we can sing their songs, we should be very pleased, not hoping to improve on them.

2

Technology, Precursors, Resistance

This summer [2010], your book *Christian Ethics in a Technological Age* appeared. Large parts of this book are very critical, not so much about technical products (say, email), but rather about the assumptions underlying the technological project. One of these assumptions, obviously, is the desire to command, to be in control, to manipulate. But, then, this desire also occurs in places we do not immediately associate with technology. For example, you write: "To define Christian ethics as concerned with a system of moral rules represents a return to a 'technological' mechanism that attempts to distill aspects of God's action in order to make them manipulable."[1] So, what is technology? Everything stemming from that human, all too human desire to play God?

It helps to remember how the story of technology begins in the Bible. The Fall narratives climax in the story of Babel, in which the biblical authors emphasize that a technical innovation made this feat possible, the invention of bricks of a special hardness. It was this innovation that sparked the idea to build a tower to God, suggesting that humanity had reached a level of technical sophistication that made God a superfluous hypothesis. If we read back from the Babel account we see that various innovations like the stirrup, music, and empire were invented by the children of the fallen Adam and Eve. Think now back to the very beginning: the first thing that happens

1. Brock, *Christian Ethics in a Technological Age*, 223.

after the Fall is the production of a material artifact, the fig-leaf loincloth. Jaques Ellul in *The Origin of the City* has brilliantly shown how modern technology is the repetition of this gesture. Unable to admit the guilt of our fallen condition, modern society can be read as one highly ramified attempt to assuage the feeling that we are missing something by trying to provide for ourselves without reference to God and hiding the disastrous results of our previous efforts.

I have discussed the problem that we sinful humans are prone to try to justify ourselves and so to displace the role of God in our lives. We want to take responsibility, be adults, not have to rely on anyone else. Think about the recent talk of "creating artificial life" in the news. Honest scientists know that we can't create life, but journalists still look for excuses to say that scientists have done it, and the public is duly fascinated and intrigued and sometimes morally outraged. But why are such exaggerations so tempting? Modern humanity *wants* to think of itself as being able to have such control of life. We feel better thinking that we could. This is the fig-leaf reflex. Am I proposing some naïve romanticism and suggesting we don't have to take responsibility for ourselves?

Wholly relinquishing control can be naïve, of course. But remember that God replaced the fig leaf with a technically superior coat of animal skins. Do we dare suggest God has stopped caring for human needs in this way? We can begin to glimpse where we might start to look for alternatives by noticing that it is possible to manage ourselves to death, to so control everything that freedom, spontaneity, and trust become suspect. Our world is a managed world, full of the responsibility that makes trust unnecessary, and it is, ironically, this management itself that is becoming most dangerous for human life, as is made clear in the most obvious way by the nuclear threat we find ourselves under and climate change. My main interest is to hold open the possibility that the rule of the Spirit and the lordly activity of Christ might offer more and better life than utterly efficient human management can offer.

To what extent is *Christian Ethics* a sequel to *Singing*? How do you see the relation between the two? If my suggestion in the previous question makes sense, then would it be too simplistic to say that the technological project is basically antithetical to Christian moral deliberation? Is technology (as a mode of thinking) Augustine's earthly city, or the tower of Babel, as opposed to Noah's ark building?[2]

2. Ibid., 227.

Despite appearances, things are actually the other way around: *Christian Ethics* was written first, but *Singing* was published first for purely logistical reasons. *Christian Ethics* began life as my doctoral thesis, but after writing *Singing* in Germany and taking up my post in Aberdeen, I continued to think as deeply as I could about our developed societies while I revised *Christian Ethics* and finally sent it off to the publishers during a sabbatical at Duke. I've been thinking about the problems addressed in *Christian Ethics in a Technological Age* while watching how new technologies enter and change our lives for about twenty years now, and in that sense, *Singing* is an inset poem within the larger project of *Christian Ethics,* answering the question about where we should go with the frustrations of modern life.

It is certainly clear to me that some of the technical problems in modern moral theory that I discussed in the previous interview are tied up with the habits of mind that characterize the inhabitants of a technological age. If you want to eradicate disease or "fix" the environment, you need a methodical plan. And if you want to do the right thing as an individual you need some moral rules, or at least rules for moral deliberation (as John Rawls has so well and influentially encapsulated this updated version of Kant's moral program[3]). I've already indicated some of the ways in which these approaches to technology and ethics parallel dominant academic sensibilities about how we can best ensure that our biblical interpretation is accurate and productive. The problem, however, arises when these well-oiled methods of thinking run up against a technology that the world has never before seen. This presents not only a practical problem, but a problem for the whole of modern ethical theory.

Christian Ethics begins with this problem, setting it out in as much detail as I can manage, and *Singing* tries to reconceive ethical theory in the wake of this problem. In short, Noah did not build the ark because he thought the moral rules of the day demanded it, nor because the technical state of the art demanded he build the "next generation" animal-carrying ship in order to make sure that his family survived in a stormy international economic environment. We are forced to ask: then what rationality did demand it? I think the answer I've tried to give in both books is that Noah heard that if he wanted to continue living with God then this is what he had to do—so he did it instead of saying "I want to make my own way" as did Adam, Eve, and the Babelites. Christians call this faith in the Trinitarian God. Although Scripture does tell us that a few concrete instructions were

3. Rawls, *A Theory of Justice.*

included in this divine direction, there is no hint, as there is in the story of Babel, that this is "new" technology. Right from the outset of the biblical story, then, the value of "new" technology is questioned in a way that is fertile for our contemporary attempts to grapple with it today.

One of the key words in *Christian Ethics* is "perception": what matters most is how we perceive the world, and to ask how Scripture can alter our perceptions. This very much reminds me of Stanley Hauerwas, who makes this point again and again. More generally, it struck me that in the recommendations you offer in the concluding chapter of your book, you seem to have moved very close to the exercises in "perception-alteration" that Hauerwas offers in so many of his essays. But if I am not mistaken, most of the Hauerwas references in your book are rather critical. So, how do you relate to his project? Obviously there are differences between the two of you, especially in style and approach. But at the end of the day, it seems that both you and Hauerwas insist very strongly on the need to speak in biblical language about our everyday moral behavior rather than relying on the "secular" discourses generally available to us. Also, both you and Hauerwas agree that Christian language is learned in the practice of worship.[4] What I like both about Hauerwas and about your second book is that they want to speak in biblical language about the most "ordinary" things, such as the industrially farmed meat I previously mentioned. So, again, how do you relate to Hauerwas?

It is impossible to overstate Hauerwas' importance both in North American academic theology and in my own biography. He directly and essentially single-handedly challenged the general disdain with which traditional doctrinal theology was viewed in a university context dominated by modern liberal theology. He did it with humor and insight and often in direct frontal assault. He reshaped the discipline as a result, and his accessible writing style at the same time provided the catalyst for young pious believers to imagine that theological thinking in the academy might matter in a way they had not been able to for several generations in America. As a result, he drew a large swath of young blood into a theological landscape that he rightly says had been dominated for several decades by establishmentarian aims and sensibilities.

4. Brock, *Christian Ethics in a Technological Age*, 249.

Medical ethics, for instance, had fallen a long way from its early roots in Christian theology, and had come to be dominated by Kantian ethics of principles. It is still the case that the majority of its contemporary practitioners, if they refer to themselves as theological thinkers, are operating with an explicitly "religious" or perhaps a "Judeo-Christian" ethic. I cut my teeth in this discipline and found its understanding of Christianity to be a pretty pale and distant caricature of my experience of the church. That's why I was stunned and immediately converted when I first read Stanley's *Suffering Presence*. It turns out that my subsequent career has not moved on very much from this book's basic sensibilities, even if I now believe that a different set of conceptual tools better reaches the point he was straining in a very creative way to reach long before disability theology had grown up around the questions he was asking. But remember that he was way ahead of his time, asking questions that nobody else was asking, and doing so in a very hostile environment. Having done so for so long he has collected a lot of interesting people around him, and I'm part of that frothy mix in my own way, though only indirectly because my intellectual formation took place in very different contexts.

Suffering Presence is a book about disability, medicine, technology, and the church. It was an unspoken homage to that book and another of his essays that John Swinton and I subtitled a book we edited *Why Science Needs the Church*. Swinton and I share an interest in the theology of disability, and it was Hauerwas who independently, and in very different ways, inspired us both. So my being in Aberdeen, in a roundabout way, had to do with the network of connections that Stanley has created with his life and work. Incidentally, Swinton and I are also heavily involved in various disability-theology projects with Hans Reinders of the Free University of Amsterdam, another academic given room to breathe in the informal Hauerwas network. When I was on sabbatical at Duke last year I taught a class with Amy Laura Hall that also orbited around related themes. Stanley's work on liturgy and ethics also inspired a young German named Bernd Wannenwetsch to come to Duke for the better part of a year over a decade ago, and so again I discovered one of my main conversation partners in the network of relationships around Stanley.

One of the things that is so fascinating about Stanley is that he is not actually trying to draw all these people into his orbit; they just end up there as fugitives from the dominant intellectual regimes, and Stanley loves to talk to new people. In fact, when I was a graduate student, it was Stanley, among others, who sent me to Britain. He has a lot of sympathy for the pre-modern Christian tradition, but doesn't work directly with it much. Following his own advice to take the tradition seriously meant coming to Europe where the historical knowledge of the Christian tradition is much deeper and so more accessible to the student. On this point I decided to follow Stanley's advice rather than his example.

On the topic of perception, I certainly learned its centrality in Christian ethics from Stanley, but I think I learned how to speak about the ordinary with biblical language first from the simple Bible-believing Christians I grew up around. I was only later taught how to understand the ways Scripture can capture and reshape perception by reading Karl Barth as mediated by my wonderful secondary doctoral supervisor Colin Gunton.[5] Stanley also gave me common ground with my other main teachers through his emphasis that choosing the right words is all-important in Christian theology and ethics. Though I first learned this Wittgensteinian linkage of words, perception, and action from Hauerwas, it was Michael Banner, my primary doctoral supervisor in London, who really helped me to understand the full implications of this claim, showing me how sociological observation can open up all sorts of theological questions by revealing the genuinely stupendous gaps that often exist between what we say we are doing and what we are actually doing. This tutelage on the linkage of words, perception, ethics, and everyday language continued and deepened when I went on to study with Hans Ulrich in my postdoctoral work in Germany. Ulrich, an old fashioned German philologist, exponentially deepened my appreciation of the theological importance of these linkages, and taken in the round, remains the modern theologian I most want to be like when I grow up.

In short, my various criticisms of Stanley are only possible because I have been so deeply influenced by, and remain so reliant on work he's done. In fact, I just came back from a year-long sabbatical spent at Duke, because I wanted to get to know him in person and see him in his institutional context before he retired. Having met him many times before, including hearing his Gifford lecture on Barth at St. Andrews, I was still amazed and humbled at the time he spent talking to me during my sabbatical year. But I also wanted to know him personally because in the years to come the most important trends in the field that I will have to deal with will in many respects be reverberations of ideas and emphases that Stanley put in motion.

5. Brock is here referring to lectures later published as Gunton, *The Barth Lectures.*

He has a lot of students and has made plenty of enemies, and given that I am in fact in neither of these camps, it seemed important to have as deep a knowledge as I could of the man himself in his own context. Also, being from Texas and a bald white man, I do worry that at some point I'll be saddled with the expectation that I should be the next Hauerwas, and so I have avoided some of his more famous modes of self-presentation. To take one example, I never say "I'm a Texan" as an identity marker in the way he does. I have indicated why I think the identities we claim for ourselves matter, and why too much interest in the activity of self-naming is itself problematic. Stanley and I had long discussions while he was writing his memoir (which I read as a late draft) about the way he portrayed himself as a bricklayer and a Texan, and only ended by saying, "I discovered I'm a Christian." I'm a Texan, but I've never been under any illusion that it is an ontological category, which is a very Texan thing to assume. If anything, I'm certain that saying "I'm a Christian" demands that I consider what it might mean to say "I'm a recovering Texan." I hope I'm transparent enough to myself to be able to admit that all of this is probably the long-winded way of saying that though we are, in my view, doing some fairly different things theologically, I remain tempted by, and in *Christian Ethics* may have succumbed to, an uncharitable Freudian impulse of sons to emphasize how they are different from their fathers.

In the acknowledgments of *Christian Ethics*, you devote a few sentences to your son, Adam. You may not want to elaborate on this, but if you are so inclined I would like to ask: has your understanding of technology been changed by the experience of seeing your child depend on such cutting-edge technology as heart surgery?

My first child, Adam, was born in Germany after the early version of *Christian Ethics* was finished and right in the middle of writing *Singing*. He nearly didn't make it through his first week. The passion and despair at the frailty of human resources to stave off death that comes through in my treatment of Psalm 130 in *Singing* is a result of it having been written during that period. Some may find the references there to Job a bit incongruous, but I could not make sense of our situation without thinking through the faith of this man who lost all his children and yet did not repudiate God.

Five or six years later I was thinking about finding an image for the cover of *Christian Ethics* that cohered in a meaningful way with the book's content. My overriding interest was in finding an image that painted neither too dismissive nor too anodyne a picture of our technological present. It occurred to me that a picture I took on Adam's fourth day of life was perfect. He is in an incubator, blindfolded, naked, with tubes in most of his orifices. Some people find such a picture distressing, and I must admit that for many years I couldn't really look at it. But Adam, being sedated, is certainly not distressed in the picture. He is in a second womb, through which he was literally born again. What an intimate love we can give to such fragile new lives today, hanging onto them against the threat hovering over their precarious existences! It is precisely the ambiguity of modern technological life that this picture brings before us in a book that is sure to be disturbing to many. It won't have done its job if it is not. In my mind that picture is half of a diptych with the famous album cover from Nirvana, in which a healthy baby is pictured in a similar blue light but is underwater in a pool.[6] The baby's eyes are open, and dangling in front of the baby is a fish hook with a dollar bill on it. In both pictures it is quite clear that humans are largely helpless beings: sometimes on their back and comatose and being kept alive by technologies, other times head up, but immersed in technology and in that environment always chasing money with all the strings it entails.

We didn't know it at the time, but Adam has Down syndrome, and now has autistic characteristics. The latter may be a result of brain damage he suffered during his close call that first week, and it is not out of the question that it might have been prevented by a more scrupulous application of medical knowledge and technology. He is now six years old and non-verbal, not yet toilet trained, and so on. Some of his challenges are no doubt effects of his brush with death and the invasive techniques modern medicine used to keep him alive. Would our lives be easier today if such technologies did not exist and Adam had gone the way of all such children for millennia? Undoubtedly. But they would also be much poorer. My wife Stephanie is a neo-natal nurse, so none of these processes were new to either one of us, and in that sense Adam's wonderful arrival didn't change my view of technology, quite the opposite—what I had written about technology helped me understand what I was going through at the time.[7] I continue to write about our life together, because as a friend who has a severely disabled brother

---

6. Nirvana, *Nevermind* (1991).

7. For an account of this period see Brian Brock and Stephanie Brock, "The Disabled in the New World of Genetic Testing."

once said to me, Adam "has disabled me." Adam exposes our technological habits for what they in fact are. As Hauerwas is fond of saying, people with disabilities are "canaries in the coal mine" who let us know when there is not enough oxygen in the air to allow us to survive. Adam is a citizen of a world in which most people test their pregnancies before they agree to care for the child that has been conceived precisely so they can avoid having to parent people like Adam. What he allows me to see in ways I never could have otherwise is how badly our modern world is set up to welcome the non-efficient and unproductive, how incredibly far it is from a world that can really receive "the least of these."

Why are eating habits and sexual practices[8] such important themes in your book? Are these also the themes that, in your assessment, should be addressed in sermons, in catechetical instruction, and so forth?

The main reason I hone in on practices of eating and sexual practices in *Christian Ethics* is a technical one. If the question of Christian ethics is "How do we receive God's sustenance?" then feeding and fertility are obvious answers to that question. This first question together with a second, "How does God rule human society?," brings the church and politics into view. I am increasingly attracted to the tradition of tying these emphases together with the doctrine of the three estates (or in the original German, *die Drei-Stände-Lehre*), which consists of the *oeconomia* (the household economy), *politia* (the political realm), and *ecclesia* (the church). I read this triad as indicating the three core aspects of human life that God has promised to care for: the realm of the sustenance and reproduction of life, the realm of political governance, and the realm of communication with God and with the saints. If Christian ethics is not a quest to find the right rules by which to live, then it makes sense to me that it is about discovering how to perceive and respond in praise and gratitude for the provisioning and ruling in which God is already involved. This is the ultimate basis of my criticisms of contemporary Christian ethical theory, that it renders God far too distant from these very practical concerns. So yes, if we are worried that the church is dying and has become irrelevant in the West, then we ought to be talking in church about faith as something that we do with our bodies. Because we don't want to be contentious in church, we doom the gospel to practical irrelevance.

8. Brock, *Christian Ethics in a Technological Age*, ch. 8.

As we Western Christians reflect on our technological age, what do you think we can learn from Christians in the southern hemisphere? For example, I would not have been surprised if, at some point in your book, you had quoted the Accra Confession, which deals explicitly with "our sin in misusing creation and failing to play our role as stewards and companions of nature."

Here is where my question "Who are my contemporaries?" really starts to hit the ground. In *Christian Ethics* I make several references to the wisdom of non-Western or non-modern agricultural practices. Western agricultural "progress" has not yet reached everyone on the planet, meaning that some people's ways of procuring food is not contemporaneous with our Western industrialized forms. So of course we still have things to learn from those who haven't yet started to do things in the manner of our industrialized agriculture. But it is not clear to me if the Christians in those places see this agriculture as valuable. They may well see it as "primitive" and tied up with the old fertility religions that they have left behind. There is no doubt that part of the missionary appeal of Christianity was that the power of modern technologies came with enlightened religion, and this was true from the beginnings of Western imperialism. So it may be that the role of some in the "dying" church in the West is to brake some of the progress of the Christianity we have bequeathed to the Two-Thirds World. We need to be able to care about them as brothers and sisters in Christ, and precisely on these grounds to warn them against covetously aspiring simply to be like us. This self-critical relation, and the braking effect it might have on the tendency of people in the Two-Thirds World to jettison their native cultures when they embrace Christ, is perfectly compatible with their teaching us what it means to rely on the law of the Spirit.

The problem of Western mission is again of a piece with epoch-thinking: it assumed the West was the "home" or "mature" church offering a packaged gospel to create "young" (read "dependent") churches. So not only does our Western Christianity divinize our Western cultural habits of looking down on our parents in the faith, it causes us to look down on global Christianity. We will always have things both to learn from and to teach other Christians that we may meet because the whole church is given the one gospel. But we can only make such an assertion because the canon of Scripture is essentially fixed, and as such exists as a divinely provided place to hear the gospel in order to become contemporaries in more than a superficial sense. Because the canon is fixed we have a place to gather and

35

think together, a place that dictates the form of our dialogue such that, in order to gather there, we have to agree that we want to somehow be like the saints that Scripture depicts. The formation of a Scriptural canon can be referred to as a "technique" (in the most appropriate sense) in that it is designed to keep people talking together and understanding one another through successive generations. But it will only serve this traditional function if we expect it to do so rather than freezing that process of transformation by taking the stance that says, "Wow! Those people back then believed the craziest things!"

Going back to your question, I generally resist the language of stewardship and companionship with nature because of the way that language is (mis-)used today in affluent Western Christianity. I would only consent to using that language if we began trying to understand what it actually means by discussing the implications of the twist in the story of the prodigal son that the "good" brother, who is clearly the good steward in the story, comes off as more than a bit self-centered (Luke 15:11–31). We would then need to look into why Jesus commends the "shrewd" steward who self-centeredly cheated and twisted arms of debtors to keep his job (Luke 16:1–12). Starting with these biblical examples of stewardship would help us to more seriously engage with the way stewardship language is used today in the Western churches in a manner that is best characterized as an unreflective divinization of economic efficiency by the bourgeoisie and wealthy, and therefore tends to exacerbate the older understanding of "having dominion" in its more interventionist formulations.

In your theology of work, you follow Barth in claiming that for work to remain creaturely, "it must remain communally attuned, reflective, and playful."[9] Although I very much like this chapter—Barth's exposition on the Sabbath is one of my favorite passages in the *Church Dogmatics*—I could not help but wonder if this offers any guidance to Christians whose work and working conditions are by and large defined by their company or sector. I mean, you and I, working at a university, are perhaps to some extent in a position to arrange our work so that it can be something like reflective, communally attuned, and playful—but how many others are? Those who own their own businesses may try, of course, as did those late nineteenth-century Catholic craftsmen who have become known

9. The quotation comes from ibid., 303; the question of work forms the theme of chapter 7 in that book.

as "corporatists" for trying to imitate the medieval guilds as a Christian alternative to nineteenth-century capitalism. However, as a rule, such experiments have little chance of survival in a competitive, capitalist economy. So, if we want to avoid "romantic images"[10] like those of the Catholic corporatists, how can we realize something like reflectiveness and playfulness? Perhaps we cannot do more than to engage in Foucauldian micro-resistance?[11]

One way I have responded to this type of question is to point out how much the modern division of labor so characteristic of capitalist societies has removed all initiative from the vast majority of workers. Even secular management theorists are recognizing that the drastic division of sheer manual labor from creative work has significant drawbacks and are trying to reverse the trend in various ways. One answer, then, is that, yes, we have theological reasons to question the Taylorization of labor, that is, our tendency to assume that everything will be cheaper and faster if we reorganize it as an "idiot proof" assembly line. My aim at this point is to say nothing more than that Christians have good reasons to take these alternative proposals seriously because they question problematic labor practices that are dominant in modern industrial societies, and which are being forced in their most draconian forms on nations that wish to join the Western market economy.

We only have to look at the vast asymmetries between the lives of those who produce Apple iPads and those who consume them to get a measure of the issues at stake. Christian theology suggests a reconfiguration of our ideas about "efficiency" in a manner that lets human beings have more of a say in how their own work is configured. Once this line of thinking is opened up, one discovers that sensitive interpreters of modern design and manufacture as it actually occurs have pointed out ways that we can make much more space for human initiative and creativity in modern work, but most of these solutions, though they make the lives of the workers better, are considered financially inefficient and so are not seriously considered. I

10. Ibid., 306. The question here refers to the discussion in ibid., 382.

11. The French philosopher Michel Foucault extended the definition of politics far beyond the idea that political engagement is reducible to casting votes in elections. Having described the ways that modern governments rule by teaching citizens to internalize rules to govern their behavior, Foucault suggests that political engagement must begin at the level of an individual's self-understanding, by trying to learn to speak and think differently and to explore suppressed potentials of our bodies.

want to broaden theologically the ways we think about the relation of work, money, and the good life in order that so-called "financial inefficiencies" may, viewed from another angle, emerge looking a lot more like modes of loving our neighbor. Part of that task is to point out that the dream of industrialized work can never entirely stamp out zones in which workers are allowed to take some initiative. Without these marginal zones and spaces, however small, micro-resistance itself would be impossible.

This is to open up larger questions about the role of government in fostering the common good. You and I work in institutions that are subsidized by the state, protected from the capitalist forces that might radically reshape what we do. We feel this in a special way in Britain, for at the moment the trajectory that Margret Thatcher opened up to think of the universities as private enterprises is finally beginning to produce academics who, once they get into "management," feel it entirely appropriate to receive business-style performance bonuses, since they are steering what they think of as large corporate entities. But this cultural transition, which is by no means complete or uncontested in Britain, totally reframes what counts as "productive" scholarship in their research and teaching. In the same way many churches (especially in North America) have lost the theological vocabulary even to notice that education is one of many sectors of our societies that are not well served if treated as a money-making enterprise. The narrowing of the vocabulary of modern Christian ethics has a lot to answer for in fostering a state of affairs in which even believers can no longer articulate the legal and ethical differences between governments, charities (which universities in Britain have been for centuries), and businesses.

Finally, speaking about this micro-resistance: I was struck by your remark that "Such resistance is rendered *more* faithful because it is more patient by its knowledge that sin has already been defeated by Christ."[12] Are you suggesting that we are forgetting the work Christ has already done if we, for example, radically break with certain forms of technology? Is a call to withdraw from certain sinful sectors of society (the world of high-risk finance, for example) the equivalent of a "frustrated call for total revolution" and incompatible with Christian patience and dependence on God?

No, it is not. The conceptual and practical problem is that modern Christians are again caught in a vicious polarization that presumes we either

12. Brock, *Christian Ethics in a Technological Age*, 384.

have a Christianity that protects the status quo or a Christianity that stands as a "contrast society" that is *only* doing its job when it is opting out of the system. Both positions are partial truths. I want to hold both trajectories together, and I think this is truer to the many biblical stories we find in Scripture than either pole taken on its own. Since I already mentioned him, think of Samson the judge bringing down the palace of the Philistines. This is Israel rebelling by breaking the systems of the age if ever there were such a rebellion. But what about that first judge, Moses? His revolution was to institute the patient business of sitting in court, judging disputes. This is the guy who killed an Egyptian in a fit of anger, so sitting in court all day couldn't have suited his temperament very well. But his service in the kingdom demanded setting up the settled institutions of judgment. In hearing and obeying this divine word I dare even say his hot-headed character was rounded off and made suppler, but it is pretty clear from the story that he didn't sit in judgment over Israel in order to develop his character, and if it changed his character, the biblical writers do not think this is a theologically interesting enough fact to tell us.

Michael Banner once responded in a debate about the permissibility of just war in this way: "As Woody Allen once said, 'some day the lion may lay down with the lamb, but the lamb sure is going to be nervous.'" His point was that it is a foreshortening of the Christian history of faith to say "all Christians believe in pacifism" or "all Christians believe in just war." Christians have been, and I would argue should be, on both sides of that problem of human life, the problem of war and injustice. The Christian soldier and the pacifist can never forget that what they do is only intelligible given the tensions that the witness of the other sets up. Nor can they claim that Christianity is ever solely behind the status quo or some relentlessly radical questioning of our cultures. The gospel is always both questioning everything and pushing the governments that exist toward continuous incremental reform because Jesus is both an incarnate God who must live as creatures do in times and places, and also the resurrected God who is not ultimately bound by the laws of nature and culture that we think we know, but is their ruler. In both moments he is radically for human life both as it is and as it will be. I would therefore like to support both the micro-resistance that can admit, for instance, that modern finance is torn by problematic practices and assumptions and into which a little Christian thought and practice could make a major difference for vast numbers of people (such as by rejecting the bonus culture, or fostering micro-credit initiatives in the mega-banks). I would also like at the same time to see Christians involved in more thoroughgoing and experimental forms of resistance as we see, for instance, in the Occupy movement that swept the globe after the financial crash and Christian movements like New Monasticism in the United States, which is trying to recover for Protestants the core monastic virtues of stability and poverty that have always been present in Christian monasticism since Benedict of Nursia (fifth entury AD). Unfortunately, I think the academic discipline of Christian ethics has tended to impede rather than foster thinking of the Christian life in these terms in being, by and large, trapped in the belief that Christians must be either conservatives *or* radicals. In Jesus, I believe, we see that God is always a partisan for concrete human lives, and as this love is lived out it constantly has to resist both the conservatives and the radicals who collapse the important tensions bequeathed by Jesus with their ultimately ideological insistence on a single set of policies. We could call Jesus a conceptual radical and a political iconoclast—which is simply to say that because the world is fallen and hurting, at no time is God for the simple maintenance of the status quo—though we may not yet be clear what needs to be overturned and what preserved about the current arrangements of our societies.

3

Environmentalism, Teaching
Theology, Nationalism

From your perspective as an academic addressing moral and practical theology in a secular university, and within a largely secularized society, what are two or three critical challenges you face in engaging students in discussions related to their environmental ethical responsibilities as citizens in a modern democracy?

I'd begin by saying that, unsurprisingly, student opinions in the UK can be quite different than opinions in the US on a range of topics, and the level of environmental engagement would be one area in which I think the nuances would be noticeable. To start with, in Britain, however amorphous their understanding of all sorts of the mechanics of the science and policy debates, it would not be only a convinced minority group, but the average student would hold a pretty strong moral position on environmental questions. Most students would assume that a commitment to environmental responsibility is an unambiguously good thing and one that governments and individual citizens should be concretely addressing. On this point students are reflecting a political consensus that has allowed the UK government to push through much more drastic reductions in greenhouse gas emissions than the federal government has been willing or able to do in the US. Students' feelings of responsibility might not necessarily be strong enough to lead them to forgo a plane trip to lie on the beach in the Mediterranean, but they wouldn't thoughtlessly buy those tickets, nor would they think it meaningless to raise a moral question about their having done so. My colleagues in philosophy and I agree that one of the easier classes to teach in ethics is environmental ethics. There is a trailing wind on that topic. And my impression is that the moral landscape has different contours in North America, especially the further south you travel. Obviously that's a very broad generalization, and there will no doubt be howls of protest from some American Christians for my having made it, but by and large I think it holds.

Having just had a sabbatical in the States two years ago (2008–2009), my experience suggests that by European standards, US undergraduates are relatively less engaged in discussions of more systemic questions. What seems quite clear is that in public discourse generally there is a firmer consensus in Europe that ecological issues, especially carbon and greenhouse gas emissions, must be dealt with and therefore that the core issue is ensuring that the means to reaching these goals will be publicly debated. Part of this consensus is reflected by the fact that in the UK it's assumed among students that this is really *our* issue, it is the issue of our age, and it will be us who will have to do something about it.

This sounds similar to the way in which youth in the '60s understood Civil Rights as their generation's responsibility, and also at least the germs of the environmental movement. This era was marked by a more critical assessment of the impact of multi-national corporations rather than holding to environmentalism as a benign good among many others. Would you then see a parallel here with the way theology students in Scotland view environmental issues—as priority issues for their day?

Yes, I think this is a good parallel. This priority is again tied up with a much stronger cultural momentum that would include things like churches tending to have a display at the back of the sanctuary or a special week relating to environmental issues. This will have been the case for at least a decade, if not three, in most churches. My background presumption is that certain moral issues stay alive when churches and other communities are in agreement amongst themselves about what counts as a moral issue and what does not. In Scotland, as in the UK and Europe in general, right across secular society and in the churches, environmental questions are simply assumed to be important and far reaching. That is not to suggest that this shared moral sensibility extends very far into how it is that we ought practically to respond to the issues at stake. But at the moment the task is to come up with concrete suggestions and to flesh them out, not to argue about whether environmental responsibility is a legitimate or pressing goal at all, as it is for so many in the United States.

That's why, broadly speaking, my day-to-day engagement with moral issues has to do more with tying that inchoate moral sensibility together with more concrete questions of a theological and real-world nature. For instance, is carbon trading an appropriate expression of ecological conscience? Is it the only thing we are talking about when we're trying to discharge this moral onus we feel? Is it a mark of environmental responsibility, understood as a Christian, to pay the additional twenty pounds when we buy that plane ticket? Is that what we are talking about when we talk about environmentalism, or is there more to it?

As we explore the role you hold as a moral theologian preparing the next generation to be not just a presence of good but a force for good, could you comment on the political side of students' ecological commitments? Democracies cannot exist as popularly elected benign dictatorships, though that's quite often the way that parliamentary democracy is characterized in Britain. So it's interesting to hear that you see environmental issues as ones that are engaged quite consciously by your students and in the context of a democracy that allows them much less in the way of incremental engagement beyond casting a vote for one of the major parties once every five years.

I don't think I would put things precisely this way, because the grassroots movements associated with environmental questions have been pretty strong in the UK for some time. I'm not quite sure how you're reading the problem of the reduction of politics to voting only every five years. This sounds to me much closer to the US situation in which so many environmental issues are resolved at so many governmental levels and through so many backroom deals that it is easy to be demoralized and depoliticized. In comparison with the US, the Green Party is relatively strong in the UK, sometimes even getting their candidates on ballots, and even stronger in continental Europe where Green politicians regularly take seats in various levels of government. In a sense, voting for the Green Party does not deal with the problem of the undifferentiated nature of representation in modern democracies, because voting for the Green Party means you have to embrace a whole political platform. But the fact remains that in Europe in general the diversity of parties seems to indicate a richer pallet of living political positions that looks remarkably more diverse and therefore less totalitarian than a two-party system in which all the really important decisions are made in caucuses.

How would you see the grassroots movement in Scotland relating to the less visible place of environmental concerns in parliamentary democracy here? I gather you see that as a somewhat helpful counterpoint culturally? Could you expand upon that?

Well, Iona is in Scotland and the Iona Community movement originated here. The whole Celtic spirituality movement is strongly tinged with environmental concerns and has a good following in the Church of Scotland as well as the Church of England. Even in comparison with the post-Christian New-Age crowd, which is still a fairly small percentage of the population, the Iona movement is a vanguard in continuously keeping questions of creation care in the foreground. I know previous generations of Scots were, for instance, very morally engaged in the anti-nuclear movement, and some still are today. If we go further back in history we find Scots like John Muir, who as you know was the founding father of one of the most influential conservation organizations in America, the Sierra Club. Similar cultural trajectories continue in the relatively strong interest, for instance, in the local food growing movement, which is especially attractive as most of Scotland is relatively remote from the major population centers. There's a more obvious economic rationale for thinking about these sorts of initiatives, including renewable energy initiatives in Scotland. More than 80 percent of the UK population lives in England, leaving much more space and agricultural land in Scotland. This also means there is more latitude to keep alternative arrangements going because direct government is more open to such experimentation up here, I think. There's enough countryside available for people to work with, and there's a supportive enough regulatory environment to give it a go.

There remains, then, a bit of a frontier mentality that allows people to not feel so tightly overseen by the UK central government in Westminster on agricultural issues, land use, and land access issues. The stripping of Scottish rights to grazing on the commons by English landlords in the eighteenth and nineteenth centuries (called the Highland clearances) remains a viscerally powerful cultural memory. Westminster is not going to tell *us* how to use our land. This sentiment meshes well with the anti-supermarket protests that occasionally occur all across Britain. In Bristol they recently had a riot about a Tesco supermarket going in. Just to the north of Aberdeen there is a consortium of farmers who have a farm shop where local produce is sold, and it is well supported by the local populace. But the last time we talked to the guy who runs it, and asked if he could point us to the pick-your-own strawberries farm that used to be nearby, he replied, "The supermarkets ran those guys out of business."

And so there are so many levels at which these issues both need to be and are being thought out, that I'm not sure it's quite accurate to say that people feel like their only choice is at the point of voting for their national government. The city and shire councils do have quite a bit of power over what goes on in any given region. And people with ecological concerns are certainly taking advantage of that freedom.

Despite Mr. Trump's success, in which the Scottish national government overrode the decision of the shire?[1]

Yes, I think so, even though it is clear that there is an inter-Scotland, inter-regional conflict, as in most places. That conflict is especially evident in Aberdeen because, per capita, it is the richest city in Britain, but at the same time it is the northernmost medium-sized city in the UK and so tends to be seen as the hinterland. Also, because there is so much oil wealth, more tax revenue goes out to central government than comes back. In the context of local government, this fact is usually mentioned in order to excuse closing down homeless shelters or schools or as an excuse for not fixing potholes, a situation that is only inflamed by humiliating interferences, such as the first minister of Scotland overruling a local planning commission's decision.

Do you think this situation bodes well for the sense of student engagement? What does this mean for those who are about to complete their education and who will very soon be thrown into the political life and the environmental concerns of the community? Preparing students for

1. Scottish First Minister Alex Salmond's intervention in the planning process for Donald Trump's golf course is depicted in Anthony Baxter's feature length documentary, *You've Been Trumped.*

this transition would seem to be an important issue for facilitators like yourself, who are shaping the moral sensitivities of the next generation.

You are certainly right that people tend to feel disempowered by the political system as a whole. Local involvement helps diffuse people's frustrations, meaning that certain kinds of environmentally engaged activity can actually be an important outlet for expressing what might be considered more classically political activity.

Let's consider as an example of this point a local Aberdonian called Ian Wood. He made a fortune of hundreds of millions in the oil business and is one of the top twenty wealthiest Brits. He wants to replace the big sunken garden in the middle of town, a last remnant of the seven valleys over which the modern city of Aberdeen is built. As it now stands, it is a striking valley right in the heart of the city. Wood has put up £85m if the city will match it and approve his idea to cover up the valley with a big structure, making it level with the surrounding city. It's the classic millionaire's vanity project, which will both be a monument to his "largesse" and will reconfigure the city in a way that makes it easier to shop in the city center if you live in the shire and drive in it every day by car.

You have to keep in mind that the city center was kept alive as a shopping area because it was built up and maintained for decades by the fact that people had to ride public transport to get there. It was the place where the train and tram lines, the port and the bus line met, and for none of those was parking needed. But the oil wealth of the city has made it possible for far more people to own cars, meaning that they will either need to build shopping centers outside of town to which they can drive (which is happening to a certain extent) or they will need to increase the access of car drivers to the shopping that currently exists in the city center by making parking easier.

On one reading the proposal to replace the garden in the center of town is part of the re-engineering of the city as a car-friendly city. Like all medieval cities built on hills and furrows, it's not really a car-friendly city. Martin Ford was the shire counselor on the planning permission commission who cast the deciding vote to refuse permission for Trump to begin building his proposed golf course development (which as you mentioned, was overturned by central government).[2] As a member of the Green Party

2. Martin Ford has recounted his role in the tale in his "Deciding the Fate of a Magical, Wild Place." He appears to have had prophetic foresight in spotting the incompatibility of Trump's vision, linked as it is with the fortunes of the hyper-rich jet set, with more

he has continued to be a central player as part of a strong minority who are very vocal in saying that Wood's vision is not their vision for Aberdeen. They are resistant to the lack of transparency that is tied up with oil barons deciding what's best for the whole city.

So what is called the "City Garden Project" has really become a lightning rod issue in the past couple of years. In my view this is an environmental issue because it demands everyone think about how the transport infrastructure of a region is configured, and why it should be configured in one way or another. The issue has both garnered a lot of interest and raised concerns that are probably long overdue about the lack of transparency in the political process in local Aberdeen politics, which, as you can imagine, are dominated by the major transnational oil companies. One of the other institutions of higher learning in Aberdeen (Robert Gordon University) does an annual survey of political attitudes in Aberdeen. This year they reported that they're seeing the lowest rates of voter confidence in the political system for thirty years because the city council has been supporting the Garden Project in the face of very obvious popular objections.[3] Somehow or other it seems obvious that Wood has influenced the city council. Ironically, the city council made their own bed by supporting a privately sponsored opinion poll on the topic, which asked people what they wanted with "their new gardens." What do you want? Do you want a fountain? Or do you want green space? Or do you want a concert venue? Or do you want cafes? And there was one little box at the bottom, Do you want it at all? And the majority, over 50 percent, checked they didn't want it at all.

So not only had the powers that be spent the money to make up some plans and do the survey, but they now had to ask the PR guys how to spin it so that it didn't look like the defeat it was. All this was going on while the council essentially privatized the garden so it could be overseen by a different committee with fewer open meetings than the city council, and on which almost all the seats were held by business and moneyed interests. Now decisions about the garden have been taken out of the arena of public responsibility and it has been made a private venture so it becomes an

---

holistic concerns about Aberdeen and its people. Having already bulldozed the wildlife area on which the golf courses were built, Trump later threatened to abandon the project if a recently permitted offshore wind farm goes ahead, and this in the face of a local economy seeking to use its position as the "oil capital of Europe" to gain a foothold in the green technology market. See also Ward, "You've Been Trumped," and Crighton, "I'll halt £700m resort plans over turbines, warns Trump."

3. Calum, "Councillors 'damaged public trust,'" 9.

investment option for consideration by elected officials but largely planned by private parties, limiting the need to appeal to public consensus.

In the end frustration with the process yielded a housecleaning at the most recent elections, with the previous council being voted out. I think this clash is both symptomatic of the clash between the culture of oil and the culture of ecological concern as well as a clash about what it means to have a democracy. We see such clashes all around the globe, if not so openly as the one I have just recounted, in which the wishes of big business and finance and their desires for named projects, legacies, and heritage projects meet and are in various ways resisted by those who dream of more organic developments of cities that take into account more rounded considerations of whether we should still be committed to being cities organized around the car or not. In my view these larger cultural clashes are what fueled this particular political dispute, and will no doubt fuel many more to come in the many places where our current ideas about energy, cities, and building have not yet really taken into account that the age of oil is drawing to a close.

This brings us nicely onto the topic of the engagement of moral theology with such disciplines as city planning and strategic thinking as distinguished from political engagement that culminates in the refusal of some debated proposal. It suggests an alternative political ethic that asks more concrete and constructive questions. We might say, for instance, that we want government to be working to preserve the following services, we want to uphold the following priorities, and that these are every bit as important as building hard surface structures. Maybe we want to preserve cobblestone streets, not just because they have an historic character but because they have survived for several hundred years and have preserved water tables by allowing rain water to percolate down through the structure rather than generating dirty runoff, which then overflows our sewer systems. We might engage in a whole range of strategic debates and allow people to become more directly involved in a manner at once more local and more far reaching than the politics that once every five years chooses one of the national parties in an election.

Returning to your role as a facilitator directly engaging with this generation, and with the awareness that there are these types of direct engagement available below the radar of national politics, which is very much part of the culture that you are immersed in—how do you approach

those young people in the course of your direct contact time with them? Do you broadly expose them to the methodological approach, do you directly challenge them on material questions, do you attempt to engage them in activist-type research or projects as students? I would be interested in how you move from moral theology/philosophy into pragmatics.

At the undergraduate level, my most obvious answer comes in the form of the course that I teach called "Exploring the Tradition of Christian Ethics." In that course I take the students through some main works of major thinkers in the Christian tradition, or at least as many as I can do justice to in twelve weeks, which is only slightly more than twelve thinkers. We start with the New Testament and the Didache, then Clement and Tertullian, and then Augustine and Benedict, then we jump up to Thomas, then we go to the magisterial Reformers (both of them), and Kierkegaard and Nietzsche , and then into a couple of modern folks up to a contemporary or two. I'm doing something like what evolutionary biologists describe with the phrase "phylogeny recapitulates ontogeny"—I am letting them face and think through the turning points and layers of questions that have brought the tradition of Christian moral thought to its current form. I want students to get to walk through pivotal moments of the development of Christian thinking as participants, so that by the end they can read contemporary texts against a backdrop of what Christians have thought in order to get there. In my experience this way of teaching Christian ethics is fairly rare. And the only reason it works (and this is a long windup to answer your question) is that I never let them just read their source readings as simple historical texts confined to their historical age. I always ask them, "What do you make of this?" and "How do these arguments connect to your world?" I'm constantly bringing up contemporary questions to get around our modern tendency to read our predecessors in the faith as if they were sealed within the confines of their historical era.

A core aspect of the task is teaching students how to analyze moral language. Because I think that's really one of my main tasks, to help them understand how moral language connects to life. Several weeks ago, just two days after the killing of Osama bin Laden, we were discussing Barth's account of what it means to be part of a nation. The text suddenly came alive because some of the students were disturbed about the celebratory dancing in the American streets. So we talked about why they were disturbed. How do we think about nationalism, and what does it mean to think theologically about this question? How do we theologically construe our "we"? With what language do we properly name our allegiance to some group of people? And why *this* group of people? The nation state is a pretty recent invention, right? Why isn't our clan or village the locus of our visceral allegiances? This line of inquiry allows students to start to think about how everyday concepts and moral language carry a ton of freight behind them, freight that will push and deeply shape your perception and so action in ways you might not be comfortable with if you don't learn to interrogate it in an intelligent way.

Thus the question "Why I am disturbed about something I've seen?" is really an opener for my interest in pushing students toward some sharper analysis and deeper self-awareness. What is nationalism? For a theologian such a question ties into a theological rationale very tightly, because Israel has a picture about what nationalism means—now we can bring in what we've been reading about Barth's analysis as to what Israel's account of nationalism might mean for Christians. Once you've had two hours of that discussion students go away thinking about the moral claim of their own nationality, having been provoked by a German-speaking Christian who had painful experiences of the moral claim of his nationality in the context of both world wars, who had been kicked out of Germany for his lack of national allegiance, and who was writing out of the middle of the strong nationalist rhetoric of the Cold War. Should there be an American in that class who later hears a political leader say that the moral claim demanded by their nationality is, for instance, to send in the military in the service of national energy security, or safety from terror, or to save democracy, these discussions immediately, I hope, will allow a non-standard set of questions to be asked. Ultimately, that's my facilitator 's role: to allow theology to generate a different set of questions.

While we are on the point of nationalism, in these classes it is also always an international crowd. I almost never have just Brits. My undergraduates used to be mostly Scots with a smattering of students from the continent. And now we're getting more English students, along with an American or two, and maybe a continental student, sometimes an African. I also tend to invite most of my first-year graduate students to sit in on the class. I find this cross-cultural ferment to be very pedagogically fertile. We are all prone to assume that the way we think about things and the way we do things is basically the way they should be done, and so when we start to think about so many areas of our lives, such as government or international relations or even family structures, we very often end up deploying theological reasoning to justify what we already know or do.

When you look at older ethics books this tendency to project local morality as universal morality is quite obvious to us, but it's very difficult to grasp the ways our own moral certainties may well just represent the prejudices and presumptions of our own peers. I do take the students through texts that expose and conceptually analyze this problem (such as Friedrich Nietzsche's *Genealogy of Morality*), but this is a problem that simply cannot be addressed only at a conceptual level, at the level of theory, but must be something that we existentially grasp in our lived lives. If we are thinking about these things *in the midst of* living in another culture, or *with* people of other cultures, the concept that much of our moral thought is self-justifying takes on much more concreteness. We learn in very detailed ways how some of our moral certainties, even if all the Christians in our home culture would agree with them, are probably not certainties for which we can muster any serious theological defense. If we, not only students but I include myself, are willing to embrace this challenge, rather than retreating to defensively shore up our assumption that the way I/we do things is best, then we are forced to think more theologically about our presumptions, and must let the moral certainties we have imbibed from our age carry less weight in our moral universe.

This is why, for the time being, I believe it is part of my vocation to be working in a British university, training many American graduate students, because it is very hard to do good moral theology if you've never had the experience of being pushed outside of the bubbles in which we never have to think very hard about our moral presumptions, and the US is certainly one such bubble that is particularly sturdy because of the wide diffusion of the English language and American imperial dominance. The senior Roman Catholic bishop probably had the right idea when, during the height of the Cold War battles over political control over Latin America, he advised Ivan Illich that despite their role in shoring up American government maneuvering, American missionaries should be embraced as offering an opportunity to "speak back" to American Christians.[4]

This lesson is, however, one that I think is important for anyone who wants to think in any serious way about Christian ethics must learn: that

4. The actual quotation reads, "I was prepared if necessary to dedicate my efforts to stop the coming of missionaries to Latin America. His answer [that of Bishop Manuel Larrain, the president of the conference of Latin American Bishops] still rings in my ears: 'They may be useless to us in Latin America, but they are the only North Americans who we will have the opportunity to educate. We owe them that much.'" Illich, *Celebration of Awareness*, 25.

we need to be alienated from what we think we know in order to genuinely grow. On this score ethics is a very special discipline, pedagogically speaking. We can only study ethics in the midst of lives shot through with moral beliefs, and in comparison to the knowledge of calculus or neurology that we might bring to a university course in those disciplines, we know quite a bit about the moral claims that we take seriously, and we probably hold some of those beliefs very firmly. If ethics teaching, then, is to get anywhere at all, it must begin with unsettling some certainties. That's why I begin my Traditions class by breaking the students up into groups and having them try to come to a consensus about the relevance of the biblical passages that are called the *Haustafeln* that recur in the New Testament ("wives submit . . . slaves obey your masters"[5]). These passages recur in Scripture, are very obviously ethical in scope, and are difficult for us to deal with given that the cultural and moral parameters have changed on every one of the topics that they cover.

Only when students realize that, on closer inspection, they are not really too sure how to connect their belief that the Bible is important for Christian ethics with their moral presumptions are they ready to travel the road that Christians have traveled since the first century. How do we know *which* text is relevant for an ethical discussion? How do we read biblical texts as part of the *canon as a whole*? What is the role of *theology* in this process of reasoning? In what ways does Christian thinking draw on or engage with *secular* thinking? We can take each of these questions in turn by reading the works of Christians wrestling with them down through the ages, and this approach has the added advantage of familiarizing students with the sorts of material moral positions that Christians held along the way, and the way they understood Scripture and their place within the church.

In my experience this approach avoids the danger of teaching ethics as "information" that can be memorized, or as a survey of positions that need to be learned in order to be certified as some sort of expert in the field. A historical mode of introducing ideas allows students to appreciate that certain concepts were forged in the face of lived realities and questions, and therefore may be criticized for being incomplete while at the same time being quite clearly an advance from earlier ways of thinking about a given topic. It allows them to see that moral claims are always developed in the face of local problems, and that they are ventured as a particular sort of

---

5. The most extended texts are in Ephesians 5:22—6:5 and Colossians 3:18—4:1, but several shorter versions also appear in the Pastoral Epistles.

faith-act. They are not rational deductions from some supposedly clear eternal truth or truths. Most importantly, having broken down the process of learning into discrete segments, the student has the chance to really learn what it might mean to think with and within each concept, so gaining the confidence that what they are learning is not just ideas, but a capacity to understand how they work in, and are constantly related to, daily practice and moral language.

One criteria of a facilitator is the ability to enable others—in this context your students—to know how to access information accurately, and that includes acquiring a historical perspective, and as you've described it, knowing how to unpack language. Could you address in more detail the other component elements of your role as a facilitator with regard to postgraduate or undergraduate students? We've already discussed how students are introduced to texts and arguments from traditional thinkers and can learn about their ideas not just to immediately apply them but also to appreciate the historic weight that comes with them in order to think intelligently about how this will shape their own thinking, or even their ways of framing what the ethical question is.

At the same time, you have highlighted that there is an opportunity for pragmatic involvement beyond being involved by voting every five years. Given what you've said about the below-the-national-political-radar opportunities for politically relevant engagement and the ways in which you've framed your role in the value formation of your students, how do you see this carrying forward then into political activity or legislative or community action issues? And how do you engage students in that whole process while they sit in a classroom?

Let me just continue from where we left off, and say that I understand myself first as a theologian. My core job is to teach students what counts as a theological argument, not to take them to demonstrations (even if I do see them there sometimes!). I will have failed if I let them through my class without having taught them that just because they're a Christian or sympathetic to Christianity, and they have a moral belief, that doesn't make it a Christian belief. That doesn't mean it's wrong, it just means that they don't know if it's right or wrong, Christianly understood. I think that my main role as a facilitator is to teach students how to take basic creedal claims and see the connections between those creedal claims and Scripture and the Christian tradition of engaging that material to make sense of moral claims. Take this conclusion: "You should quit burning coal." This moral conclusion, which has quite practical and wide-ranging implications, can only be reached by way of a set of claims about what it is that you're doing when you quit burning coal. Common sense may know that the smoke chokes us. And though that may be right, it's not, on the face of it, a theological claim. You need to do some work on how a doctrine of creation, for instance, undergirds the value of bodily life in order to say that certain behaviors, the way they're being carried out, result in the destruction of bodily life. I want to teach students to be able to engage well in arguments with those basic presuppositions.

Something telling happened to me recently. There was a huge, brand-spanking new anti-aircraft warship moored in the harbor in Aberdeen, the HMS Diamond. Surprised to see it, I remarked to my wife Stephanie that it was a pretty imposing beast. She later quoted my expression of awe at it on Facebook and one of my students from the Traditions course a few years ago wrote back to her. He said, "I'm surprised he said that, because he's a pacifist." Now I'm happy to be confused with a pacifist, and I'm not sure that's an inaccurate label, but I'm certainly not a garden-variety pacifist. I hope that my Christian beliefs don't make me a garden-variety anything. But the fact that my own student wasn't precisely sure what my position was is intentional, because I want students to understand how to think as a Christian, and that doesn't necessarily mean to think like me. I'm edging here toward a later aspect of your question—the modeling aspect of it—which is a constituent part of my job as an academic and as a church theologian.

A footnote to that point is that I think I am a church theologian who, because of some accidents of history, works in a university. I do not consider myself a university scholar who has a special interest in this subset of universal knowledge called theological knowledge, nor am I designated by any official church to head up student engagements in social action such as protests. Ultimately what I think I'm doing in the classroom is teaching the future teachers of the church how to negotiate questions that they won't learn to negotiate if I just tell them what the answers are, and this holds true whether they end up working in academic settings, in pulpits, in some other sort of ministries or even as Christians in various workplaces. This breadth of vocations that my students will take up shapes how I approach my teaching of Christian ethics, because in the many different walks of life they will take up they will face moral questions from an incredibly diverse set of positions, and I work hard to ensure that I give them what they will need for all these different Christian lives.

There is a time and place for many types of different ways of being Christian in the world, and the discernment of the times is a constitutive part of what it means to be a Christian. So I'm not trying to teach them a moral package of conclusions, or to suggest that this or that ethical crusade is what Christians ought all to be about. I'm trying to teach them to recognize what counts as an argument, that this is the time and the place for a given action, to aid their own discernment. I can't teach them what only their own discernment will be able to tell them, that this is the time and place for X or Y action. And I've learned from the tradition of Christian thought what I mustn't teach them: that there is always and only one right Christian action that must be done no matter the circumstances. This is not a relativistic or perspectivalist account of ethics, but a recognition of how much damage has been done by modern Christians when they have assumed that we can act well in every situation if we have in hand a set of moral principles or actions we believe is sufficient for anything that might come our way. Life can throw plenty of situations at us in which we are not sure how the balance of considerations will come out and so are forced to act in faith. I want to teach students that such circumstances are not so rare, and acts that respond to them are also not "blind" faith, because we can intellectually discuss how faith operates in situations that are so morally complex that we are not sure we even know what the right thing is to do.

So there is a cogent way forward to arrive at a point of discernment, even though the end result may vary from generation to generation, given the broader cultural context. Nevertheless, the pattern of discerning thinking is one you hope to convey, not as a set of packaged conclusions, and not by offering a prototypical formula, but by helping students walk through the process, sensitizing them to the constitutive elements of a healthy process of discernment. Would you recognize a need for there to be congruence between what you are facilitating and how you model that as a facilitator?

Let me take that in two directions. One of the reasons I quite like the opportunities offered by the British academy is that I'm not expected to be a public intellectual in the sense of regularly appearing in big press outlets or being asked to speak on the radio, even though the things we discuss are very much the topics on which the newspapers would like quotes from an ethics lecturer. It is easy for academics to get into that game if they want to, but at the moment it's not something that interests me terribly. What I am interested in is teaching students one at a time or in small groups, because I think that the most important learning goes on when we are working from the solid real world knowledge that students bring to the table. There is a kenotic aspect to teaching, a Christ-like lowering of one's self in order to be where your students are that differs from blasting them with erudition in a great salvo that withers them and makes the academic feel smug. When teaching becomes the downloading of a whole packet of conclusions or information a different sort of knowledge is produced than when you say, "What do you think?," and use a more Socratic method. This also differs from speaking to the media, offering a "position" in the either-or culture of contemporary media, and from speaking to large groups. I'm interested in serving as a midwife for knowledge of a certain type; my remit is a very narrow sort of knowledge. But I do believe that the contemporary church badly needs the sort of knowledge I help her to develop.

At the most fundamental level I think this is a political stance and models a political perspective. I say this with something like Sheldon Wolin's political theory in the background, specifically his claim that democracy as we know it in large industrialized nations is ultimately suppressive of politics, because politics in the most fundamental sense is based on genuine consensus building.[6] To teach students in a secular university what it means in practice to find a consensus is both to support the university as an institution that lives off trust, and democratic society that does as well. We see examples of governmental attempts to circumvent democracy understood in this way all the time, most recently in the UK when the government formulated an explicit strategy to suppress a wave of anti-nuclear sentiment in the wake of the Fukushima accident.[7] This observation is particularly important in relation to environmental questions because on issues with such wide-ranging import as environmental ones, governments in industrialized societies have every reason to suppress dissent and therefore the building of any real political consensus. Think about what would happen to energy policy if environmental concerns about fracking, for instance, were allowed to play a serious role in the political process.

6. Wolin, *Politics and Vision*.

7. Edwards, "Revealed: British Government's plan to play down Fukishima."

I therefore agree with those who regard the basic position of governments in modern Western democracies as typically managing from the top down. My wanting to speak to smaller groups is related to reversing this situation by seeking to build types of consensus from the bottom up, by tending and grooming an appreciation for deep conversation, with all sorts of different peers and with the saints who preceded us. Every week I have each student write a page response to what they've read. I'm very intentionally trying to have them fly their own colors and then talk about that among one another. I think, in theological terms, that is what democracy has to be. It does not spring from a political theory of rights or a political settlement like a constitution, but from a notion of the communion of saints and the consensus that must be found amongst members of the one body of Christ. I don't think Christians have practiced consensus-seeking of this type for several generations, or even seen that as something we need to work on, which makes it a hard skill to develop in the face of apparently benign structural arrangements that thwart careful, honest, and genuine converse of this type, even in universities.

In political terms, then, I see my modeling and my teaching as, in an odd way, very heavy-handed. I set up the atmosphere in which people have to display their own position and work through their own position together, and are forced to take account of the opinion of the guy over here who is trotting out the garden-variety Tory position, versus the person over there who's championing the Liberal/Scottish Nationalist position, and the African student who is concerned about quite different issues than either. I find it both obvious and exciting that you have to do theology to even start to have an intelligent discussion between these very different positions. What's at stake here? How do we even ask the question about what is at stake here? What surprising thing can we hope to emerge from this activity? One of the real eye-opening moments on my sabbatical in the US was the realization that there has been a remarkable decay in the ability to find a way to discuss positions that are conceived in very oppositional and polar terms. So I'm just trying in one small forum to teach people what it means to negotiate political and moral differences *as Christians.*

That's my core responsibility as I see it—to teach students how to think and speak with one another as Christians. Nations can tear themselves apart by losing the skills of negotiating alternative positions, as societies have done and will continue to do. All I can do about that as an academic and as a theologian is to try to live out in a practical way what it might mean to enact the certainty that the church is the true *polis*, the source of our determinative citizenship. The Trinitarian God has established this polity in order to confront and work through the divisions of society, digesting them through the processes of reconciliation. And so we should thank God that in our class there is someone over here who is on the left, and over there is someone who is on the right. Because both are tenuously connected enough to this tradition we call Christian to think "we have to work this out somehow," we have special reasons to hope that something exciting will emerge through engagement. We need to relearn how to hope in such a forum, to enter encounters hoping to be surprised, ultimately, by God, but through the insights of another human being. And even though the class-room setting is semi-artificial because it is not strictly speaking a forum of the church, students will have to deal with one another or at least people who hold their positions after they leave this place. If I've offered them a non-threatening forum and taught them what it means to have a discussion about a contentious issue that they share with non-believers, I hope they will have learned to draw on their shared theological beliefs, and later will remember that they have that tool set at hand and will carry forward the hope to be surprised that sustains genuine politically generative converse.

You've raised another provocative point. I gather from your comment that you would also like to see that thinking permeate not only local churches but also the broader ecumenical community of faith, which can then serve a sort of seasoning or exemplary role in political life. I gather, then, that you see this as a crucial contribution that can be made by the Christian community in a secular context. Given that you're using the classroom as a crucible in which students can gain experience in building this kind of consensus, what does it mean that you are doing this in a secular university?

I learned a lot from my own doctoral supervisor, Michael Banner, now at Cambridge, who spends a good deal of his energy in government committee work. Before I was even a PhD student, he was, at a young age, the Chair-man of the Home Office Animal Procedures Committee, between 1998 and 2006. And he's been on the Human Tissue Authority for five or six years, appointed by the Secretary of State for Health, and has in the past dealt with questions like what to do about CJD, the disease of the brain related to mad cow disease that can spread in hospitals because it is not destroyed by the normal sterilization procedures for surgical instruments. He's written a fair bit about what it means to be a theologian working in that kind of context, and one of his main lessons is that in a public context you don't have to make theological arguments all the time. You do, however, have to know what a theological argument is and to know what your own position is.[8] This is the origin of my attempts to teach my students to ask, "What is a theological argument?" I hope they learn this even if I don't always have the time to teach them exactly what it means in specific discussions that the theologian is not compelled to trot out an explicitly theological argument.

In my view the discussion that's often had about keeping religion out of politics is relatively uninteresting. Religious or quasi-religious beliefs are all over the place, and of course drive people's policy formation, but none of us argue our positions in public debate beginning with deepest beliefs at the first go. That's just not how political converse works. So I think the bedrock of Christian public engagement is knowing what and how Christians think. You need theology to show you the relevant distinctions, and those distinctions allow you to see things, which means that theology is in fact always helping you to think and frame questions even if you don't explain on every occasion where those distinctions come from and what makes them important. Once these basic priorities are clear, there are all kinds of tactical decisions to be made about how you might engage with particular discussions and what sort of arguments you might make. That's another layer of the assumptions built into my own pedagogy.

If you're talking with legislators who take positions A, B, and C, sometimes you just have to go through in detail why A, B, and C, taken on their own terms and premises, are pretty problematic. You don't necessarily have to always make explicitly theological arguments, or even make explicit constructive policy proposals in the course of political negotiation, though this would be the ideal. That's a perfectly acceptable way for Christians to engage in public life. Also, given the way my own understanding of what counts as a Christian argument is put together, I can't necessarily presume that my own prejudices about any given topic are correct. There's a healthy self-suspicion built in all the time.

The upshot is that in a secular university like mine, one just has to go along and see what the people studying transport, city planning, or renewable energy have to say, what their alternative universes are. You have to go along and hear the folks who specialize in the history of the oil business. I

8. See Banner, *Christian Ethics*, 26–46.

mention the latter because it can help in thinking practically about energy policy to know how badly politicians in the UK have managed the North Sea compared to how it might have been done, such as in Norway or Shetland where the windfall of oil has all been plowed into the State finances in a canny manner. It takes a little bit of political awareness and engagement to think about how the whole energy infrastructure has been set up in the past, based on specific political decisions that might have played out in very different and much less denuding ways. Knowing this history gives us a much better sense of what we might do, and where we might push today if we care about seeking more sensible energy architectures. A big part of what it means to be a Christian in the public and at a secular university is to just go hear what people say and realize that you can learn something, that just knowing how to make moral arguments does not necessarily qualify you to make the real-time discernments that public policymaking demands.

Another one of my teachers, Hans Ulrich, is very good here as well. He showed me how a theologian can just go and listen to people working in their own field and bring to bear their analytical and theological skills to pick out aspects of the way they are seeing any given topic, in order to interrogate them both to learn something and teach something. The reality is that most moral questions are decided on very mundane grounds and in very mundane contexts. You don't even know what the mundane questions are that are morally relevant until you've had a pretty extensive discussion.

The best place to look where I've worked on this sort of thing is a report that I wrote in *Disability and the New Genetics* on a conversation that I was part of in Germany between Hans Ulrich and an eminent molecular biologist named Walter Doerfler.[9] Given the vast changes afoot in how we think of the human being and the ways medicine is being driven by discoveries in genetics, it is important to work out what genetic biologists actually know. They're the ones who define genetics as we know it. What do they think is clear? What do they think is not so clear? Where do they think this whole experiment in intimacy with our genetic heritage is going? What do they think they're doing? You can address these questions as a theologian. But you'd best not, as ethicists tend to do, tinker around with worst-case Frankenstein scenarios that are attention grabbing, but are probably miles away from the moral questions that are being faced in the lab as we speak. That's shoddy ethics, in my opinion. I don't really know what is happening on the ground until I've talked to people who are doing

9. See Brock, Doerfler, and Ulrich, "Genetics, Conversation and Conversion."

the thing on the ground. So training students to understand Christian ethics is teaching them how to listen. As they listen they need to know how to spot the theologically relevant moments in a discourse and then to begin to unpick what is at stake in those theologically relevant moments. I hope that in this process the church both becomes more articulate and sophisticated about what it thinks about any given topic, and in a manner that allows the "world" to become more articulate and sophisticated about what it thinks it's up to as well.

I'm not a zealot or an activist in the sense that these titles presume a great certainty about how the world should be. Christianity is neither a validation of what everyone agrees is the right thing, nor is it the overarching vantage point from which the highest aspirational ideals can be seen and preached even as we assume that nobody will ever completely realize them. I am summarizing Reinhold Niebuhr's position here, which is dominant in the Christian ethics guild in North America and is usually described as "realist." I see myself as being more interested in realism in the sense of getting into conversation with real people and taking their beliefs seriously, not in the sense of having a theory about how best to make compromises when we can't live up to the ideals that Christians see exemplified in the life of Jesus. I want to learn from people in a large university, and Aberdeen is a great place for that because it is big enough to have lots of interesting things going on, but small enough to make extended conversations with other academics easy, as well as with professionals outside the academy. Both in private and in public I try to take advantage of that rich opportunity for cross-disciplinary discussion as often as I can.

Every once in a while when giving a paper to non-theologians I've had very funny introductions, like, "I've looked at this guy's CV and he really is a proper doctrinal theologian. But he's going to talk to us nonetheless." I think giving people outside theology that kind of shock is salutary, so they see that theology doesn't equal a sort of esoteric expertise. Of course, there are theologians who try and keep the walls up, or even work to keep them up. And, much to my chagrin, in general theologians working in the secular university either give away their own ground saying something like "we don't have our own discourse, we're critical thinkers or social scientists of a certain type," or they learn to say, apologetically, "we do have our own language, but that language is not one that's cut off from anything in the world, even if we can't make all the connections."

If you boil down what I think is important about working in a secular university it's that in it you will run into Christians who realize that Christianity isn't a ghetto, and theologians have no need to pretend that their knowledge set is irrelevant to most people's lives. I mean, plenty of Christians are scared off by a secular university, but I think it's a real opportunity, because the church exists in and for the world. Doing theology in a secular context often reminds you that secularity itself is less freed from the legacy of Christendom than it often assumes. Avowed unbelief and understanding belief cannot be directly equated with the divide between those who say they are not Christians and those who identify themselves as church members. There are many things supposed secularists hold as tenets of faith (some of which were formulated by Christian thinkers, for Christian reasons) and there are many ways Christians talk faith, but trust reason. Christians rightly pray, and should pray more often, "Lord, help my unbelief."

I consider my classrooms and interdisciplinary discussions little hothouses in which the church and the world can talk in a sustained way in order that both can discover what they believe in, to take stock of their poverty, and in the face of that knowledge to think hard about where they might make a contribution. At their best in such forums we can begin to see the relatedness of many different realms of life and begin to learn how we might draw on the lessons learned by people who faced similar situations in the past. Most importantly, in such contexts we can learn to hope to be surprised and to discover what we share that will allow us to make practical progress together. Too often and on too many topics Christians have little to bring to the table in such discussions, and universities are too infrequently configured to value such conversations. But God does have something to give to us in the concrete configurations of our societies. The church needs to discover what those always surprising gifts are as much as the world needs the church to know who that God is.

4

Energy, Mobility, Economy

Please identify three examples of dilemmas in environmental ethics that, in your opinion, have received inadequate consideration, the consequences of which are now having a negative impact on the culture.

A theme I'd be interested in discussing that falls under this heading is energy. How should we conceive of the ethics of energy extraction and use? What is the moral and practical landscape within which we begin to think about such questions? Here we will need to discuss ideologies of growth, oil, and rising energy costs, which is relevant if energy costs are going to go up markedly in the next ten to twenty years. This will put a lot of pressure on lifestyles as currently lived in the developed West, which has become comfortable with a lifestyle formed in an anomalous moment of energy profligacy if set beside the patterns of energy use in every previous period of human history. One reason for this is the way that mobility is built into the fabric of contemporary society. The dilemmas this infrastructural organization forces on moral thinking have not been seriously engaged in a theological manner. To do so would require specifying what we mean when we use the term *energy*, what we are actually implying when we presume that Christians are for growing economies, mobile workforces, globalized manufacturing, and commuting lifestyles. Despite this lack of serious theological analysis, plenty of Christians are in favor of these things on grounds that they believe are Christian. That's why raising the question, "What is energy and what we are doing with it?" starts to put pressure on a fabric of taken for granted conclusions across a fairly broad swath of at least North American Christianity.

There's a multitude of micro-questions lying behind these macro-questions, questions about specific public policy choices and about what we want out of the modern life and how we think we deserve to live it. Both are implied in discussions like the one Obama has touched off just this week (mid-July 2011) by saying that he wants to raise the average gas mileage rating that will be mandated of American automobile manufacturers. America is in general something like ten years behind Europe and even Asia on facing and dealing with particular policy questions like this.

Yes, they have yet to produce reasonably priced vehicles that can achieve seventy miles per gallon, not to mention per liter as you have here. Having already put people on the moon, the fact that the American public continues to accept these standards as being legitimate, on any level, says something about the power of the media. It echoes a theme you previously addressed, the way in which the ability of the individual to enact environmentally aware choices can conflict with political decisions and policies that have created an environment in which important alternatives have been eliminated.

Absolutely. You can't go into Burger King and ask for a burger made with sustainably raised beef, pesticide-free wheat, preservative-free pickles and lettuce that has not been trucked in a frozen container 1,000 miles. You also can't ask to be served by someone on a working wage, who has been given the opportunity to think for themselves at all during the day, or who has actually learned a skill, like cooking, that they could take to their homes or use to apply for a job at a proper restaurant. The fact that every stand-alone Burger King has a drive thru also reminds us that the ways we have laid out space in modern cities disenfranchise everyone who does not have access to good public transportation. There you have the dilemma of modern technological life in a nutshell.

Part of what I was getting at with the reference to Wolin's critique of modern democracy is the power of vested interests. These interests are paying lobbyists to make sure that institutions and infrastructures do not change in any way that will reduce their profit margins. This is a pretty banal or perhaps conspiratorial thing to say if we don't take the time to look more closely at how these processes concretely play out. The car manufacturers' lobby will do everything it can to undermine stronger regulations and for all the reasons we discussed in the first hour.[1] I don't think that there is one eternal Christian position on fuel efficiency law. Policy change of this type is an intervention made by politicians at a place and time within cultures as they stand. I think raising fuel efficiency standards is probably a prudent thing to do, and I think it could most likely be defended on Christian grounds. But Obama's not defending it on those grounds. Nor are Christians discussing the topic, defending their position on Christian grounds. Neither of these observations about the lack of explicit theological language in the public debates is necessarily worrying. But what is worrying is that Christians don't even know how to think meaningfully and deeply about these questions on their own grounds, that is, theologically.

Why do you think Christians would avoid drawing obvious correlative links with Christian notions of stewardship ? Is that because you see, at least American Christians, as in some sense having given theological credence to free enterprise and everything that goes along with greasing its wheels? Is the assumption that free enterprise has a quasi-religious backing?

That's certainly one big aspect of a puzzle that has a lot of pieces. The job of the ethicist is to try and get a clear sense of what the arguments are that actually shape people's imaginations. One important way to do this is simply to put Christians in the position of feeling the need to articulate a Christian reason for their positions.

A pastor friend of mine in California likes to joke, "We know why Christians drive SUVs: because it's a Christian responsibility to kill the other guy's kids." That's a humorous way to put at least one of the arguments Christian use to defend the status quo, the rather commonly held belief among Christians that the safety of our kids comes before everything else. All sorts of rationalizations for the way things are get swept under of the "it's for the kids" rug. We move out to the suburbs. We put our kids in schools away from "those" people, and we use as much fuel as necessary, since it's nice and cheap anyway, to take them back and forth. And if we're investing in the kids, keeping them away from danger, then why wouldn't we buy a car with a large crash bar in front, and so if you run into a Saturn your kids will survive. Built into the whole equation is the assumption that

1. See Chapter 3.

a Saturn driver is at least suspect of not really taking their responsibilities as a parent seriously. My pastor friend's joke therefore taps into one of the strong arguments being used to justify the status quo, and in so doing opens a discussion that can very easily lead into ecological questions. An academic version of this strategy is deployed very effectively by Amy Laura Hall in her *Conceiving Parenthood: American Protestantism and the Spirit of Reproduction,* which nails down the concrete forms in which the "it's for the children" self-justification logic plays out in relation to a range of related practical questions.

They deny environmental concerns by preferring to focus on their responsibilities as a parent?

Perhaps not deny, but certainly marginalize, sideline. My job as a parent is to get my kids to the best school I can get them into, and to soccer practice, and not to have anything happen to them in between (such as getting run over by a car while crossing a street made very wide to accommodate cars and not foot traffic). There are two obvious premises that will fuel resistance against the political mileage reform that Obama is talking about. One is the unspoken fact that energy has to be cheap for this picture of life to work at all, combined with the more often articulated belief that bigger, heavier vehicles are safer and so any good parent would want to drive one to protect his or her kids. The PR analysts for the automobile manufacturers are doing the same things Christian ethicists should be doing, analyzing the moral beliefs that support the status quo, and so they know that they can win a public discussion by shoring up this argument: they can immediately respond to Obama with the retort that the public won't buy the cars that will be small and light enough to get the mileage reductions he is proposing. And they're right. At the same time they'll be doing everything they can to manipulate the public discourse so people continue to believe that small cars like you see on the streets every day most places in the world continue to be assumed to be death traps. But the pitch would never succeed if Christians understood at a visceral level that the car we drive is part of how we interact with creation, and that this interaction, like many others, matters far beyond what it means for our kids.

A closely related set of questions relates to how compact and integrated the spaces in our cities are. My sensitivities on this issue come from having grown up in the universe of oil. In many American cities you have to get into a car to go anywhere and everywhere, and this is often worse in cities either organized around the car, like Los Angeles, or that grew up during the era of cheap oil, like most big and small cities west of the eastern seaboard. Though like commuters, for whom time in the car feels like their only "quiet time," I learned to enjoy certain things about it; in the end I found this bondage to the car inhumane. If you drive, you have to drive a lot, and if you can't or can't afford to, you are at the mercy of others, or the accessibility of public transport, or you need to take your life in your own hands by going on foot in cities organized for the car. Now that I live in Europe I've taken advantage of the privilege of living in cities built when foot travel was the norm. For the fifteen years I've been an academic I've never lived anywhere where I've had to use transport powered by anything more than my body. It just seems to me to be an obvious way to have a better daily life, and to consume less. I've also discovered that a life reliant on foot-travel has a nice unity—you come to know people outside their "official" roles, since you see the postman at the pub, and can have those who serve you in one capacity over for a barbeque at your house. I think that part of my role as an educator is to open up experiments (I use that language a lot in my discussion on technology) and try to do things differently, and to see how it comes out. And it just seems to me to be a no-brainer that if you can walk five or even thirty minutes to work, you would, even in places where the car is still king, or even better, "lord."

Might this link with the New Urbanism that originated in Minneapolis and has rapidly spread, especially to the coastal areas, so that people at the very least might welcome this insight when planning resort communities? When people arrive for their vacations they don't want to get back into the car and so they've been willing to experiment with pedestrianized villages and communities. This has given people a little taste of what life like that might be like, although not many have yet extrapolated those insights as prototypes for organizing cities. The approach to mobility in the United States today can be seen as a legacy of the Victorian period here in Britain, during which mass mobility was resisted at the level of the House of Lords because it would give the opportunity for social mobility. Americans have taken the opposite position by claiming social and physical mobility as part of their legacy. If you're going to have an ever-upward and onward social structure in the United States you must give people mobility. But that doesn't necessarily demand gasoline-powered

automobiles, or that you cannot utilize public transportation. Disney-land has had a monorail working for over fifty years that is silent, clean, and runs on an air cushion. It is electrically powered, and has worked very effectively moving millions of people in the middle of the complex freeway system in Los Angeles. Great irony. So there was our experiment, and we're looking at it, and it's working quite effectively, yet we're still building freeways.

Disney has certainly been a utopia-generator for about fifty years now, and its theme parks are direct inheritors of the World's Fairs that conceived the future in a very infrastructure-heavy way, as I discussed in my technology book.[2] The monorail was held out as an icon of how the future could be if we would just commit the resources to build it. But it is noteworthy that this is not really a vision of a world with working public transportation (signaled, not least, by the fact that the monorail technology used, espe-cially the closed loop-style tracks, makes junctions difficult to build). The Disney city Celebration signals the development of Disney's own vision of how American society should be. In Celebration, the city as a whole is engineered, and in this total city plan car infrastructure is treated as an aesthetic problem. The ideal image we have of what an American town should look like isn't covered with pavement, nor does it have a bunch of cars on blocks in front of the houses, which in fact you're going to have if everyone has to drive everywhere. The traffic problem and car clutter was always the unforeseen problem of the suburbs, and the solution we see in the planned city of Celebration is that they've tried to hide all that away through clever infrastructural design. But they haven't questioned the car culture in any serious way. An aesthetic critique of suburbia has been lev-eled, but it's ultimately not an ecological critique, and may well in the end be more energy costly.

I wonder if the New Urbanism tends toward projects that are closer to this vision than they'd like to admit, being attracted to these new build planned developments ordered by many aesthetic considerations, which cannot in themselves induce the cultural changed needed to make such planned communities thrive. By way of contrast, compare how subdivi-sions are laid out in the Netherlands, which are organized to prioritize cycle traffic. The presumption is that the majority of the population *want* to live within a bike-organized pattern of mobility. When new builds are set up,

2. Brock, *Christian Ethics in a Technological Age*, 140–44.

they are organized around the bike highways, bikes have the right of way at crossings in national law, and it's presumed in planning decisions that it is going to be best for all of us for the bicycle to be the main mode of transportation, and planning decisions enact this priority. I do think that there are experiments along these lines in the US, such as the Via Verde development in the South Bronx,[3] but I'd like to see them more intelligently discussed in theological terms, and I'd like them to focus on serving lively communities rather than aesthetic criteria. I would also like a clearer articulation of precisely which cultural changes the designers of such developments believe themselves to be asking of their inhabitants. Different travel patterns? More local political engagement? Shared responsibility for the grounds? Or is the underlying assumption that people could transplant their current lifestyles into these new builds, as the architects of Disney Celebration certainly assumed?

I take Los Angeles, by which I also denote the sprawling urban landscape that encompasses Orange County and reaches far inland to places like San Bernardino, to be a classic American car city. It's not suicidal to walk or ride a bike, but it's close to it. Many political decisions have been made along the way to yield this result. There was good, working public transportation system very early on that the car lobby intentionally destroyed. One of my earliest lessons on what can happen when government and media collapse into one another came at a relatively young age when I read a great history of the modern media in the US.[4] I was genuinely shocked to learn how the automobile and tire manufacturers had colluded with property developers and media magnates in LA to shut down a working tram system in favor of buses and cars. Political decisions have been made all along the way that, in the terms we discussed in the last hour,[5] were anti-political in being non-democratic. LA is just a particularly striking example of what happens to cities when you keep opting for the car. And it's not like unbelievers "out there" have been making those decisions. They have been made and they keep getting made by Christians based on what they think are Christian reasons. But this dream of what a city should be will only last as long as the energy is really cheap.

Having worked for a year up in the high desert (Palmdale, California), I think there's going to be a lot of ghost towns on the margins of LA in the

3. Kimmelman, "In a Bronx Complex."
4. Halberstam, *The Powers that Be.*
5. See chapter 3.

not-too-distant future. You can't drive fifty miles each way to work and pay the energy costs indefinitely. It's not executives but working people who have to live this way. LA and Las Vegas are places where we're going to first start seeing the real world impact of the assumption that energy is free. This is an expression of an historical sensibility. I'm not making a moral argument.

When future generations look back at our age, roughly between the end of the First World War and now, I'm guessing that they are going to say that the developments in science, technology, and culture that happened during this period were very important in all kinds of ways, but they squandered an incredible amount of energy. It was treated as a bottomless well out of which we could draw indefinitely and with which anything could be done. Houston is another of my data points on that story. When I was a kid gasoline was twenty-five cents a gallon and it is four dollars something now, which translates into something like seven pounds a gallon here. This is why here even driving a car that runs on unleaded gasoline, instead of diesel, is kind of looked down on as a squandering of resources. In many places in the developed world we're in the middle of a cultural evolution in which the uniqueness of this one substance, oil, is being recognized, and attempts are beginning to be made to try to wean ourselves from it, not least by revisiting our images of what constitutes a livable city.

In general my experience is that this sensitivity has not yet made as deep an impact on the larger political landscape of North Americans, as indicated by the reality that in North American political culture, the only way discussion of these issues can be approached at all is by casting fuel efficiency as an opportunity for technological development and industrial profit. The only political move open to Obama is to say that if we don't start developing alternative energies we're going to fall behind by losing out on the next wave of technological development. This will cut into our profitability resulting in a waning capacity to exert our will on international developments.

As it will over our own culture, since we'll then be subject to decisions made by those who are producing the goods, those running the governments of other countries.

Well, so far we seem to have done a pretty good job keeping producers in other countries under our thumb. There's no point being an empire and having military bases in every corner of the globe unless you can control your resources. You don't have to do much reading around about the politics of the modern Middle East to learn that first Britain and now the US have taken great pains to keep oil allies in place, using both above and below board tactics. You also don't have to know many Africans involved in the oil business today to learn that the West has honed its legal mechanisms for making sure that it controls not only the world's oil, but who gets to profit from its extraction, transport, and refining.

These are things that are much more easily seen living outside of the United States. America is a specific sort of empire. We do have hard power projection, through guns and aircraft, but our primary mode of rule is really soft cultural power, which is always underlined by hard power. But money and cultural influence can be used very effectively. In many ways you can get much further running a global empire if you refuse to say, "Hi, we're the imperial masters." How long you can keep this up is another question. I'm not lying awake at night hoping that America holds on to its global dominance, and I'm sure China is happy to take over that role as quickly as it can. Scripture is pretty clear that it is a silly question to ask whether it will be a better or worse world under subsequent empires. It is in any case theologically important to keep thinking about where we are in such world historical landscapes.

Perhaps you could discuss the political power that is associated with social mobility? I'm thinking of the connection between mobility and the political right of independence of movement and action. Such rights are still denied in countries like Russia, where you must have permission to move from city to city. As we become increasingly aware of the rise of mechanisms of surveillance, it would seem important to watch out for inroads regarding personal mobility. Today every vehicle produced in America has a tracking chip in it, which gives the owner the right to voluntarily activate it for the purpose of being monitored. This tracking function is linked to your GPS system, which you require since you can no longer open a map. Unless you want to give up GPS, you have therefore de facto agreed that you can be monitored for purposes other than those for which you initially agreed to the service.

Such technical developments are always offered as solutions to an implied threat to the individual—the threat of theft, the threat of being abandoned in a blizzard in the middle of Minnesota, the threat of

needing to get through to your auto rescue service—or the larger threats that can be thwarted if we can track down vehicles driven by terrorists. This has raised all kind of questions about the extent to which, under the pretense of security issues, we are acceding to heightened technological surveillance. Do you see this as impinging upon Christian ethics in any way?

Let's leave to the side for now the important question of the rise of surveillance in Western societies, and approach this issue by staying with the theme of energy use. We can open a related question by observing that if you fly over a city in the developed world you see an incredible number of lights on all the time. What's the obvious solution to people being afraid of crime? Put up light. We have here a nice, simple, iconic picture of the way that fear and energy play together, right? We drive to the store, and we want it to be open twenty-four hours a day, but we're worried about someone grabbing us coming into or out of the car, or taking our car, which is co-essential for our lives. And so twenty-four hours a day the lights burn in the store and on the parking lot. The globe's natural period of darkness becomes a problem because we demand universal mobility, which is energy intensive, but produces social problems, which we then solve by applying yet more energy. We do all kinds of things with light: we entertain, it provides an aesthetic atmosphere both indoors and outdoors, we advertise with it, and so on. There is a whole sub-discipline of engineering called lighting studies. This activity rests on the experience of energy being essentially free, meaning that we can do playful things with it but also are not constrained to think about its use in more creatively productive ways. We just turn on the lights or put up a camera, or insert a chip and whatever social problem can be fixed, to touch on your surveillance theme. It's like the proverbial hammer that hits every nail.

There's also the issue then of light pollution.

Yes, exactly. This is one of the points at which I believe future generations will look back upon us as uncreative and profligate. We have lived in a historically very unique period when incredibly concentrated energy resources were available to us. And what we did with it was to invent mood lighting and automatic doors and have spent evenings making moving light pictures on the walls of dark rooms projecting our fantasies about having the limitless energy we would need to travel to other galaxies. We lit up huge tracts of concrete so we could drive a two-ton piece of metal six blocks to get a gallon of milk trucked 500 miles from a factory farm. With this came an unthinkable effect—we lost the dark, producing a thing called light pollution, and generated a new set of social disorders—kids not getting enough sleep because of their phones ringing under their pillow and adults kept awake by TV all night. The whole package is absurd the closer you look at it. And finding out how to unpick that and trying to find all the triggers that hold it together is a serious task not only for an academic theologian but for all of us. Nor is it a task that can be adequately addressed all at once.

The nice thing is that we don't have to fix everything in one fell swoop. Jesus didn't burn the system down, but he asked pointed, provocative, and diagnostic questions at crucial points. Stanley Hauerwas has written a nice essay on abortion in which he tries to push Christians beyond the simple pro-life/pro-choice polarity with the observation that Christians have never taken life to be an ultimate value.[6] There have always been Christian martyrs who knew that there were things worth giving your life for. It turns out that there are Christian reasons to believe that though human life is valuable, it is not untouchable. So while the sentiment might be good, the theology of the pro-life movement often is not. In the same way, Christians should all be for caring for the natural world, but not as an absolute principle. No matter how environmentally sensitive we are, it is possible that we will eat up the resources of the planet or that its ability to sustain us will decline over time. In ultimate terms I don't think there's any way to avoid that particular dilemma.

The point, then, isn't to come up with an absolute line in the sand and say, "If you're a Christian you need to stop all of this at once." In fact, we can't stop it all at once. Given the magnitude of our situation, the problem is getting any movement at all toward changing anything. There is a noticeable gap between people who just take the surface rhetoric about how the world is seriously, what they hear in the media or in popular discussion, and people who read and listen and watch a little more closely and with more questioning. And when you step over the line from the first stance into the second, there are so many things that are so wrong in our world that you don't even know where to start. Fatalism then becomes a serious temptation. A genuinely socially engaged Christian ethic has to face this

6. Hauerwas, "Abortion, Theologically Understood."

reality and learn what it means to live, and act, as if God cares about creation and wants to meet creatures in their misery and relieve it.

You've highlighted two critical, overarching areas and you've addressed some of the micro-issues that arise under those headings. You've looked at energy, you've looked at mobility as a subset of energy. You've also looked at how Christians lack a conceptual framework for stewardship in these areas. This brings us to the issue of Christian ethics as a sort of common currency, which, it might be fair to say, we have moved away from. There was a time when ethical constructs were the common language from Sunday pulpits . . . and people spoke routinely about what was the responsibility of man, and this moral landscape was part of the backdrop that lent an important dimension to discussions that were a prelude to the colonies becoming the United States. Why do you suppose that dialogue has dropped away from the pulpit?

The short historical answer is that in America the liberal/fundamentalist split that happened in the nineteenth century ended up polarizing what Protestant pastors thought sermons were supposed to be about: either they were exhortations to social activism or to repent and be saved, Moody Bible Institute style. That split largely persists to this day. All the interesting contemporary theological thinkers see this as a false dichotomy, and are trying to overcome it. And I would count myself among a crowd working against that divide from both sides, people like my student Andy Draycott who is working with the evangelicals,[7] and J. Kameron Carter, who works at the traditionally mainline/liberal Duke Divinity School.

One traditional theological way to go beyond this polarization is to talk about how God answers the prayer "give us this day our daily bread," cares for the feeding and reproduction of human life, to talk about the practicalities of God's promise to care for political stability, as well as to ask what it means that God speaks God's Word to us, which is the foundation of the church, the third estate. This traditional theological conception can help us to parse what to ask for, and what to expect from God, and what to hope for.

For instance, in our current highly developed societies we no longer hope for the home to be connected with production in any meaningful sense. The modern splitting of production from consumption obscures the ways in which the home is by definition the way in which God cares for

7. Cf., for instance, Draycott, "Preaching: The Free Public Speech."

the reproduction of the human race, and also, ultimately, the feeding of the human race. There have obviously been many benefits to the division of human labor, including in agriculture. But we do stand at the far end of the pendulum on that topic. We think that a very minimum number of human beings can be delegated all food production. But this equation is only possible if we assume vast amounts of oil. It's adding insult to injury to try to fix this problem with bio-fuels. With this suggestion we reach the ultimate regress of having a glimmer that the problem is not having enough energy while proposing solutions that require even greater rates of energy expenditure. Growing absolute demand is a problem, and it will have to be dealt with, but to just assume everything will be right in the world if we can just find new energy sources is an amazingly shortsighted reflex.

The way moderns are continually trained to treat food as a commodity, the way we think about ourselves as consumers of food products, what we understand to count as good food, how we understand ourselves to be procuring food well and eating well, all of these topics deserve much more theological thought. In certain Christian circles a sense is percolating that having a garden might be something a Christian thinks is a good thing, not an embarrassment or something that's a throwback to the bad old days of non-labor saving devices or that we do it just to save money, but because it connects us in a salutary way to the earth.

The Slow Food movement in the United States aims to recapture a certain amount of production autonomy, a sentiment that appeals to a long New England/Western Frontier tradition on the east and west coasts of valuing the independent individual and the maximization of self-sufficiency. Scotland has the tradition of the great country estates that pride themselves on being food self-sufficient. And there is a Slow Food movement on the continent. But none of those issues have emerged out of expressly Christian perspectives. Quite often not even in tandem with them. Why would you say that is?

The only examples of alternative thinking about food production that I can think of off the top of my head all have a strong subtext of religious belief. And I say religious belief because I can think of four examples—two are Christian, one is Jewish, and one is pagan. I'm also picturing communities like the one represented by the Findhorn Foundation, or the various Steiner-influenced movements that espouse biodynamic farming. So I think I would be tempted to turn the question around and say, "Is there anyone thinking seriously about these questions who doesn't have something like a religious motive behind it?" In terms of my own knowledge I would have to answer mainly "no." I'm guessing they're out there; I just haven't had much experience with them. Those concerned to identify themselves as strictly secularist have to explain why it is that we should be concerned about the planet, or why it is that we're concerned about food. I am very interested to hear how answers to these questions are put together by strict secularists. But every time I dig around with people talking about food in this way there always seems to be some sort of notion that the creation is either a divine entity or has been given by a divine entity and therefore ought not to be squandered. I myself don't tend to use the language of stewardship for a whole host of reasons. But the sense that the material world is not at our command but is something we respond to and which makes claims on us, that seems to me to be at least a quasi-theological sensibility in the first place.

5

Intentional Community, Good Works,
Listening and Responding

Please identify three examples of dilemmas in environmental ethics that, in your opinion, have been effectively addressed within the Christian community and identify the benefits that have accrued to the larger culture.

At the end of the last interview you highlighted a subliminal value system that shapes people's approaches to environmental issues, even if it emerges from a neo-pagan sense of total immanence. I want to ask now about specifically Christian engagements that have in some way modeled a constructive environmental response, the benefits of which have accrued beyond the Christian community.

One example of a constructive environmental response to an ethical dilemma is presented by those Christians who are trying to think of cities outside of the private property/individual rights/economic expansion model and doing so with explicitly Christian commitments in view. My experience has been that whether you start with Christian commitments or not, people who care about how the material world is put together end up meeting on various topics. We will find common ground with people who think that cities should be places that work as a whole and for all their inhabitants, rather than as something like a competitive battleground in which I must carve out little spaces that I command and in which I can live comfortably while others are left in infrastructural dead zones. This push-back is something the New Urbanites are championing by insisting that we ought to aspire to making cities as a whole livable for everyone rather than spreading people out and spatially segregating the functions and demographic segments of cities.

A more ecologically oriented extension of that response to modern city planning trends has made some good headway over here in the Transition Town movement, whose icon is the city of Totnes in England but has spread all over the world. These seem to me to be genuine alternatives to preserving the current arrangement while increasing our investments in various forms of private security, shall we say. Christians attracted to the New Urbanism I would see standing on the other side of an ideological divide against Christians who would say that to prepare for the ecological changes on the way we need guys like Erik Prince, the founder of Blackwater Security, the historically important and now infamous private security company that was dominant in Iraq. Prince comes out of the heartland of evangelical Christianity and seriously understands what he is doing as carrying on the legacy of medieval Christian mercenary movements, and was hired by a Republican administration that wholly agreed with his vision.[1] Prince is at least right in seeing that the only way to keep the system as we know it running without making any changes is to make sure that no one can get over your wall. Economic ideologies that many American Christians strongly support are thus directly implicated in the way our cities and international relationships are arranged and the violence that is needed to maintain them. My student Scott Prather has brilliantly exposed this connection in his discussion of how the rich used private security firms to protect themselves and their property from the poor in New Orleans after the devastation of hurricane Katrina.[2]

What would you say to Christians who have set up alternative Christian communities? Quakers, the Shakers, Mennonites, and other groups in the United States even today have an emphasis on home and/or community productivity that engages with the outside world in a deliberate and controlled fashion. There are those who would suggest that modern Christianity must effectively embrace some such community model because of the secularization of the larger society.

1. Scahill, *Blackwater*, ch. 2.
2. Prather, *Christ, Power and Mammon*, ch. 4.

I know quite well and am in direct conversation with people who understand the church as a contrast society, which needs to be different to show the world that there is a better way. This is a resonant biblical ideal, but we also have to recognize that the church as a whole doesn't really contrast much at all, when described sociologically, especially on the issues we're talking about. If anything, sociologically speaking, it's part of the rearguard demographic on the sort of issues we have been discussing.

The caboose instead of the engine?

One of the ways I present what I do in conversations within the secular university can be expressed this way—"You are welcome to scoff at me and other Christians for being part of an anti-progressive demographic, but I specifically identify with this community, and I make all the points that you would like them to hear. If I weren't doing it, who would be? Also, your criticisms of the church need to take seriously that I also am a member of that community, which might not be as monolithic as you assume it to be."

Educating ministers and future educators is one way to engage with the problem that the church is by and large not a contrast society that presents a living alternative to the status quo. It behooves us to admit that most Christians are part of the rearguard, and try to come to terms with just why that is. I'm not pretending that the reasons Christians today support the things they do is malicious, but many evangelicals do have their political positions dictated by Fox News, which is happy to present itself as vaguely promoting a Christian ethic. There are obviously going to be moments when Fox News champions theologically defensible positions and I think as you've indicated that when the churches haven't been providing substantive teaching and discussion on moral issues the door is opened to have those discussions by Fox News in the same way different news outlets provoke the moral postures of the liberal side. But Christians often forget that they should continually be asking "Which of these moral packages ought we to take seriously, if either?" You could also say that though the liberal side of the church might not be in the rearguard on environmental issues, it does seem to have lost the ability to speak in any intelligibly theological way about many other contested issues.

I'm expressing concerns that are the backdrop for the discussions I'm trying to provoke in my classroom. I'm trying to show students how to get beyond the blunt observation that some of us agree with the best and the brightest and the most thoughtful non-believers about these issues, and some find themselves agreeing with their opponents on those same issues. How then are we going to think about these questions as Christians? My students have to come to terms with the problem of negotiating not only thinking through what we, a political entity, should support, but also through the interpersonal dynamics that come with the church's own internal processes of thinking through such questions. I'm concerned that I see precious little of that discussion going on across the churches today, which is why I would read the New Urbanism as a forum in which Christians can come together around shared concerns . . . let's just start with thinking about how our cities are put together and what kind of lives they force on their inhabitants.

Over here, the Iona Movement provides an example of how a whole range of ethical concerns can hold an ecumenical Christian community together in thought and action. It's a kind of parachurch organization based out of the monastic foundation on the island of Iona. Local groups meet periodically for a worship service in churches or homes all around the UK, and there moral questions are discussed and activist strategies formulated. They generally take positions that lean to the left of the British political spectrum and they're quite involved in activism on all sorts of issues—protesting, Third World debt, raising concerns about food production, protesting coal and nuclear usage. This does have some influence in various ways on the Church of Scotland and the Church of England. The Church of Scotland is by bulk theologically liberal, and welcomes activist sub-groups who keep in view moral questions that bother people. I think the Church of England is quite a bit more diverse, but the Iona movement still leavens many corners of the Church of England. In the North American context the Ekklesia Project was intended as a more academic form of such a fellowship.

One other movement that springs to mind in relation to this question is the New Monasticism, which is relatively new. I have had some fairly long conversations with people in that movement who grasp that the vows of traditional Western monasticism—obedience, chastity, poverty, and stability—are tied up with these issues in many ways. If human life is not about making money, how should we live our lives? Well, you need to feed people. *Oeconomia*, which means more than our narrow concept of economics and is more like "household economics," is suddenly being rediscovered as part of what it might mean to be human beings living out Christian faith. This movement entails a commitment to a place and all the social problems that might be associated with that place. They almost always start a garden and try to get people involved in learning how to grow food and come together around a shared project in a place. They start trying to bring back some of this self-sustaining sensibility that underlies the Laird's estates in Scotland, but which also long before characterized Christian monasticism, which, being forced into self-sufficiency by the collapse of the Roman empire, found itself thinking quite intensely about what it might look like to be self-sustaining in a Christian manner. This meant, for instance, that self-sufficiency could never be played off against hospitality. Environmental concerns were obviously a long way from their mind. But such communities needed to find some internal coherence and to learn how best to be productive in a theological sense, both spiritually and physically. They needed to have some boundaries, but ones that were open to the world in a structured and productive way. Being bounded (as opposed to closed) was for the purpose of being open to the world.

It's that ancient package of priorities that the New Monasticism is trying to recover in deprived neighborhoods across the US. As I understand it, the New Monasticism has four primary categories of concern, three of which we have already touched on in our previous discussions: providing food, shelter, and care, which covers anything from medical care to a place of refuge for battered women and children, to taking care of the homeless. Their fourth priority is meeting spiritual needs, which is also a form of solace. Such hospitality is only sustainable when embedded in practices of praying for the world, praying for people.

These basic types of priorities have a long history in Christianity, and have oriented a myriad of Christian communities as they tried to find ways to live more Christianly together, in relation to the creaturely world, and in relation to their neighbor. There is a structure here that can be theologically described, one might say an eschatological excess. Christianity spawns these movements because its hope for healing and reconciliation is always leaps and bounds beyond what any given society is currently offering. This is why it is important that these communities have existed and continued to exist, and that they exist with their own visible discreteness. I want to stress that these communities can never really be closed. Even if they lose the aspect of hospitality, they are still interacting with the world. They are always permeable to it and can still be life-giving to the world in all sorts of ways. I love Eric Brende's book *Better Off: Flipping the Switch on Technology*, which chronicles his eighteen-month journey with his family:

a Massachusetts Institute of Technology graduate diving into a Mennonite subculture in which technology use is intentionally kept to a minimum. As he fled from a sense that technology was driving and organizing his life he found the community he came to call the "Minimites." Through a long and slow learning process he discovered a new set of mental and physical skills and ways of living. He found himself changed as a person in ways that he could not avoid taking with him "back" into the "normal" world, which he now perceived quite differently. This is what I would like to see intentional Christian communities doing, and the more the merrier!

There was an American experiment that took place in Switzerland some time back. While you might take exception, as many have in the Christian community with the theology and philosophy of its founder Francis Schaeffer, L'Abri was one of the first post-World War II Protestant attempts at communal living. Believing that Europeans had disassociated themselves with classical Christian values—after two world wars—Schaeffer felt that Christianity had obviously failed to produce the values necessary to construct a society. He came to Europe ostensibly as an evangelist to the Europeans but quickly realized that he had no answers for them because he couldn't model and live out his Christian values. He could only talk about them academically and philosophically. This was the turning point in his life. He started L'Abri, a community dependent upon self-sufficiency and gifts sought in prayer. While you are not talking about modeling per se, you are speaking to the need for Christians to live out what they're talking about in order to give credibility to their message.

Definitely. Part of the reason that I dragged my feet rather than directly answering your question about modeling grows from a theological sense that although the priority in Christian action is the doing of good works, works that are always visible, Jesus is pretty explicit in the Sermon on the Mount that it is not a good idea to draw attention to them. In a scholarly context one question I raise with defenders of character ethics is whether they can do justice to this teaching of Jesus. There's an overlap with what we see on Facebook: the platform itself essentially demands you to be constantly saying, "Look at what I did." In an ironic way that's the inverse of doing what Jesus keeps saying in the Gospels, especially in Mark: "don't tell people what I did."

Self-promotion.

The question is, how do we fit what we call the public relations value of an act together with the fundamental visibility of human action? In my view it's not a Christian responsibility to make our good works visible. I think it's our responsibility to do good works. And I think it's very easy to fall into wanting to be culture makers or leaders of culture that has a very Pharisaic ring. I resist leadership language or vanguard language that is attractive to Christians who want to be serious about their faith on the same grounds—because it is too self-conscious about where we stand in relationship to everyone else. When people live in a way that others see as Christ-like they do not need to rely on any public relations efforts. It seems to me sociologically undeniable that contemporary Christianity is very often tempted to self-promotion.

Those are the reasons why I can't set myself up as the exemplar of what a non-exploitive Christianity might be. I have to let God reveal what that looks like for each person, and for each community, and I can only hope to serve and catalyze people listening for that revelation that can only come to concrete people in particular places. If I'm talking to someone in Los Angeles there's no way that what they need to be investing in is going to be immediately apparent to me. I'll need to spend some time with them and try to evoke their perception of how their world is put together. In this sense Aberdeen is simply a different world, and the sorts of issues Christians might get stuck into here will indelibly be marked by the cultural and moral landscape in which they're living out the Christian life. At the most abstract level we are discussing what it means to trust Jesus Christ as redeemer. But in terms of what individual Christians might do in their lives, I can provide snapshots that give hints about what the peace of Jesus Christ might mean for them, but it's a pastoral task to say, "We as a community will go and do this now." And though I do occasionally fall into that pastoral role, my vocation is not in the first instance that pastoral role.

It sounds like you are offering a different account of New Testament passages like Jesus' injunction to Christians to be a light on a hill, to not hide one's a light under a bushel, because your good works do need to be seen as both a source of encouragement and glory to God. There is something that needs to be said about recognizing the difference between acknowledging that something is wonderful, but letting the primary emphasis

remain on this good work being enabled, empowered, or directed by the Creator God, not because it points to the human being who is enacting it.

And I think if you don't take a line like that you are set up for all sorts of, well . . .

Self-aggrandizement?

Yes. And self-aggrandizement runs very nicely as a closed system, a self-reward mechanism. To use a very primal form of theological language, I think the devil is pretty pleased with self-aggrandizing Christians, who are his best public relations outfit! The great opponents of Christianity in modernity, and here I am thinking especially of Nietzsche, all in various ways repeat the comment that if it were not for the church, they would find Jesus an irresistibly attractive figure. The most powerful lever that all the freethinkers used at the beginning of the modern period to persuade people to abandon Christianity was to point out the gap between what Christians said they believed about Jesus and how they lived. The problem remains that even when we do get things right—and I do think that by God's grace Christians do sometimes get it right—we don't get everything right. Anytime you say, "this is a lovely thing that Christians are doing here," it's still human beings up to it. Send in a journalist and they will find something to embarrass this community, these individuals, and that's as it always will be. It's not for us to believe that we need to present to the world a spotless example of what Christ means in everyday life. Jesus Christ alone was the spotless one, and we can at best serve his continuing will to appear in this world. It's for us only to serve the one God's care for the world. And I think that God does care for the world, does so actively, and also does so through Christians. If Christians can escape the natural (sinful) tendency to claim God's grace for themselves, they will stand the best chance of serving this divine love for all creation.

One of the ways that you have suggested that you guard against self-aggrandizement is that you model good works, but without setting yourself up as an example of good works out of caution about the tradition of self-promotion, which is often interpreted in Western culture as part of evangelism. Are there ways in which you've learned to examine your own role as a Christian and the cautionary note you try to take into account?

One of my starting points is the insight that the creaturely realm is a far more complex place than we tend to think it is. We also know ourselves as individuals far less comprehensively than we think we do. So there's a moment that should accompany all Christian thought and practice, what modernity has labeled the problem of criticism. It is good for Christians to wrestle with a response to that modern tradition. We need to find a way to say, with Kant, that to be modern is to share the sensibility that self-criticism is a good thing,[3] while finding a way to distinguish Christian and secular forms of criticism. Christians need to find a way to say "I don't think myself into criticism; I am under criticism and reformulation." Descartes inaugurated the tradition that Kant continues, which assumes that there is some intellectual apparatus that will allow us to puncture our own illusions. In my view the starting point for an intellectually serious contemporary Christianity is the admission that this belief in the power of human self-criticism is itself an illusion, and therefore that reality, the Creator via creatures, has to break in on us. And much of my work is concretely exploring what that affirmation might mean.

In the first instance, it means that we don't get to invent what it means to be a Christian—that's just something that comes down to us. Whatever else it means to be a Christian, it first means that to become one we have to join in with some people who already know God. By definition the church is something handed down to us and which we have to join in with, a process that is visible in the New Testament as Christians work through what it means for Gentiles to conform to Israel's understanding of life with God.

I've been very struck by Willie Jennings' *The Christian Imagination: Theology and the Origins of Race*, just out last year. The surface theme of the book is race, but the core doctrinal concern is to explain what goes wrong when Christians forget that they are Gentiles. He encapsulates his diagnosis of contemporary Christianity by meditating on the Syrophenician woman who begs Jesus for the crumbs under Israel's table (Mk 7:25–40). That's what Christians are. Rather offensively to our ears, Jesus answers, "I didn't come to you," to which she responds, "but even the dogs get the crumbs." And

---

3. "Our age," writes Kant in a charter document of the Enlightenment, the *Critique of Pure Reason*, "is the genuine age of criticism, to which everything must submit. Religion through its holiness, and legislation through its majesty commonly seek to exempt themselves from it. But in this way they excite a just suspicion against themselves, and cannot lay claim to that unfeigned respect that reason grants only to that which has been able to withstand its free and public examination." Kant, *Critique of Pure Reason*, 100–101.

that's where Christianity and Christians have always to start, Jennings says. A conversation has been going on between God and a particular group of people from the Middle East to which the rest of the world is not privy. The world too comes from God, but doesn't know that without finding itself captured by this obscure people group it is passing into nothingness. That's the Old Testament story of the nations. They come and they go and they fall into nothingness, or at least they do if God does not remember them, a question that the biblical narrative does not really go very far into.

Christians, then, are representatives of the nations that have to learn what is means to pay attention to these specific people in a corner of the world, to listen in on somebody else's conversation. That's the starting point of Christianity as a movement. And it is the continuing reality of Christianity because it demands that the grammar of Christianity remain fundamentally one of receptivity, hearing, and conformity to a truth that comes to us from outside. That's also a short way of summarizing what I tried to say in *Singing the Ethos of God*. How do we embrace being made part of a tradition that precedes us? The question itself is an answer to Descartes' construal of the problem of criticism. Descartes says, "I'm going to think myself out of the situation of believing some things that are probably illusions." Christians learn through Israel and through the Scriptures that they cannot think themselves out of their illusions. But they hear in Scripture the promise that God will come to them in very specific ways. The human task of faith is to learn to open ourselves and to listen appreciatively. If we do, Scripture promises we'll be made into those who can perceive and appreciate the whole creaturely realm and God's working in and through it. That's the basic structure of my response, which I would then go on to expand by examining how this might shape the ways we live in ecclesial, economic, and reproductive contexts, and how we live as political beings.

To be provocative, I don't think that many of the ethical topics that we assume are burning questions are really theological topics. For instance, surveillance isn't a theological topic. It names a cluster of human attempts to grasp and see and survey that can be applied in all different realms. But that human attempt to grasp and see and survey that can be applied in all different realms is in biblical terms cast not as a way to peace and security, but rather as a problem, and if Genesis is correct, *the* problem: we want to have universal knowledge. New technology is another commonly used category that's not really a theologically coherent category. Part of the onus of the theologian is to offer the conceptualities that allow us to perceive entities that really exist and distinguish them from entities that we think of as real, but are somehow illusory.

We think that there is something called a new technology, but it's not a thing, it's not an entity, it doesn't have reality any more than such a thing as human races exist. We can try to convince ourselves that people with blonde hair make up a group that are in some sense superior beings, but at the end of the day this is self-delusion. There are theological reasons to put this in the strong way that I am. New techniques can be developed by human beings, but they either receive the care and sustenance that God lavishes on humanity, or they exploit that grace, hoarding and trying to keep it away from others. Coming to terms with our world as one in which things are happening all the time that are always related to their context in the economy of divine ruling and presence is part of the unfolding of the Christian tradition, in which we must learn to receive our very being.

I know this is a counter-intuitive point, but it can be illustrated with a domestic example. To learn to love a child is to learn to know what sort of noises they make when they need something, because they're not going to convey their needs in any other way. Descartes can retreat into his child-less domestic realm and believe the fiction that he can think himself into reality, but I'm proposing entering criticism from the other end by saying, "Thinking I can think myself into a clear perception of reality is an evasion of letting myself be shaped by reality." I have to learn from the noises and motions that a human child makes what it demands of me in order to become the person that I'm supposed to be, as a servant of God's allowing the human race to continue itself. That framing of the matter can be extended across all the fundamental activities of human subsistence.

In theological terms, discussions about environmental topics are scaled up versions of the same analysis. We have to learn what the atmosphere, water, and the animals tell us about who we are. As fallen beings we are prone to believing ourselves beyond reproach, or at least not as bad as we might be, and to believing that we live in this creaturely world in a manner we can defend as good stewardship under some criteria. Yet there remains a verdict being levied in the material world on our behavior by the baby who is still crying, the glaciers that are still melting, and the nuclear waste that is sitting in ponds and caves and will wait to have the last word for thousands of years if necessary. As a theological educator, my first pedagogical task is to open up people's perception to these realities. I do believe that if people's perceptions of reality change, the ways they live their lives tends to follow. My faith is that if people's eyes are opened to the world in which God is acting, if we confess to believe in a God who teaches us in the church that we need to be remade by conforming to something outside of us, then we will be claimed and remade in ways that we could never have predicted beforehand.

Another domestic example: as you know, I've had some surprising twists in my private life and that has meant that I have had to re-jig my professional life to try to discover once again what it means to be a parent in a technological world, what it means to have a child in the world who is still here only because we live in an extremely technologically invasive culture, in both the good and bad senses of the word. When you have someone in your family with leukemia,[4] you can't say to your scientific friends, "you're monkeying around with creation to be throwing everything you've got at cancer." Such criticisms are shortsighted because people who know how to treat cancer or repair hearts only know how to do this because they've paid very close attention to what the creation has told them as to how bodies are put together.

As those who believe in a good Creator, Christians always have something to learn from all sorts of people who have reflected on and learned from this material knowledge. Becoming those who are able to learn from people who have really paid attention to the materiality of creation as it reveals itself to us, or God who reveals his own creation to us, is something both Christians and scientists can learn to do if they are not too constrained by scientific ideas like Darwinism that can drift from a scientific, empirical theory into a dogmatic worldview, as we see in polemicists like Richard Dawkins. This more dogmatic deployment of a scientific theory tends to immobilize the close and perceptive attention to the material world that is the essence of science. Fostering this open kind of perception in a manner that displaces more doctrinaire and closed forms of knowing is one of the main hopes I have for my students, because Christianity can quite obviously become closed and doctrinaire.

You are suggesting that one of the critical and positive contributions Christians might make in terms of environmental issues is to step outside talk about "the environment" as a narrowly defined topic by indicating that what we are talking about is actually an extension of a much larger

4. At the time of this interview Adam Brock, at eight years old, was undergoing the intensive phase of chemotherapy for acute lymphocytic leukemia.

account of reality that has to be embraced in its entirety. This would benefit the culture at large by encouraging the realization that technological advancement does not exist in a vacuum. Its significance has to be looked at within a broader picture that goes beyond questions about whether a proposed technological development meets a production objective or addresses an existing gap in the market or will be well received by a particular industry. This would make agitation for a wider point of view an important part of what a Christian can bring to the area of what we call new technology.

I would hope so. It's a way of approaching the matter that is intellectually and existentially coherent, but it's rare, to put it mildly. As we have previously discussed, within the contours of specific political discourses some moral appeals are allowed and others disallowed. In the contemporary US context Obama couldn't say both, "We can't keep throwing money at healthcare" and "We need to have some national solidarity at the level of the concept and practice of healthcare and about what it means to be a nation." He decided to propose healthcare reform on the grounds that we need to save money, because I think he knew it would be a Herculean task to actually convince however many million Americans to really care that everybody had health care. He knew he would have to do so against the best efforts of the lobbyists for medical insurers and pharmaceutical companies who know they can find lots of Americans who will agree with the claim that "my money pays for my health care." He knew he couldn't even count on Christians if he were to take on that argument.

All the same forces are at work over here, threatening the strong national solidarity on the issue of healthcare forged after World War II, so this is not simply an American problem. But the sheer destitution of the postwar years in Europe made it obvious that national solidarity was not really optional. That was a gift of that horrific war: people saw that they simply couldn't make it alone. That's a gift that America has not received in an obvious way, ironically, because it became so wealthy after World War II. The result is that it still very much suffers under the ideology of individual self-responsibility.

This is why the disability topic is so important to me not only for obvious personal reasons, but also because it's another way in which a wedge can be driven into so many ideologies in North American Christianity. What's the church's mission to disabled people? What is preaching to disabled people? What does it mean to live in harmony with creation alongside disabled people? All those questions have fresh light thrown on them not only as thought experiments but also as real, lived questions.

How do we really live out the church's mission if we affirm that Christ came also for disabled people? My answer connects with our discussions of the environment because although Jesus in his Great Commission does picture Christians going other places to make disciples, lo and behold, when Christians take this seriously they always end up in some place with specific people. Then the question is, What will you do and say? When Jesus talks about mission, he pictures it as a form of bringing God's life to the world—God's redemption, reconciliation, and healing. I think the mission of the church is tied up with what it means to be human, and this is portrayed in the first chapters of the Bible in the form of the four rivers that flow out of the Garden into all the world, and turn up again as life-giving rivers in Ezekiel and for a final time as the river of life in Revelation that is so powerful that it becomes a massive flood. We tend to think of mission as a post-Fall mop-up operation designed to re-inform people of something they have forgotten. But the Creator of heaven and earth seems to have originally intended that the spreading of God's caring formation of an already good creation in the form of the Garden of Eden would have in time been spread to the whole world through human labor if human work had remained oriented by God's own speech. The Garden would have been extended because God told human beings to be gardeners; that is, to pay attention and perceive and respond appropriately to what has been given them already patterned and good.

Telling the story of God and his people in this form helps to get around some of the sclerotic habits of highly industrialized Protestantism, which tends to take on board the Enlightenment's anti-Catholic aesthetic in which the bad old days were dark and labyrinthine and unhealthy and we need a new simplified clarity of the gospel. It's a vision that slots all too easily into an industrial-monocultural universe in which the church's mission is not a way of preserving what is genuine and constitutive of local places, but which tears down hedgerows in order to allow the combines to harvest from horizon to horizon. It's especially difficult for contemporary Protestants to notice when they've crossed over the line from caring for the renewal and remaking of human lives in redemption into an equation of Christianity with globalization and monoculture. I do think people now and then wake up to some specific aspect of this problem, finding themselves repulsed by, let's say, factory farming and slaughter houses, but they don't know where to go from there. My interest is in trying to find a way to exploit those isolated moments of discomfort in order to offer a more rounded and detailed vision of what it means to be a Christian and what it means to be a creature.

6

Higher Education, City Planning, Heaven and Earth

Where has Christian higher education succeeded, and where has it failed, to address environmental ethics? Broad theoretical and theological approaches may be cited as well as specific instances of practical engagement.

Let me start with the first part, "where has Christian Higher Education succeeded?" I'm not sure how broad an analysis you are seeking here, so let me start with the academic discipline of Christian ethics. There are certainly some people who are extensively engaged with environmental issues in Britain. I am thinking of the "grand old man" in this area—Timothy Gorringe, who, over some decades of writing and team building, has made the University of Exeter a hotbed for Christian environmental ethics. Another is Michael Northcott of Edinburgh and, closer to my generation, David Clough at Chester. I'm also thinking of people like Norman Wirzba and Ellen Davis at Duke. All of these scholars in their various ways are pressing far beyond the imaginations of Christians in the pews by insisting that environmental questions are important to ask and deserve theological answers. That's one answer to the question of where success can be granted to Christians in higher education.

There are a few failures that come to mind, and one of the most obvious is that even amongst the group that I have just praised there has been a tendency to—not all of them but many of them—speak about the environment in sort of an apocalyptic tone, that if we don't act now we are actively destroying the world. And other Christian thinkers, whether ethicists or not, have often responded that this is only one of many important issues—let's call this the foot-dragging approach. While granting in theory that environmental considerations are important, they are deprioritized in a way that defers taking them too seriously. A significant number of North American evangelicals are the worst offenders here, in my opinion, though there are changes afoot in this group. Having zoomed in on the field that I know best, the university discipline of Christian ethics, there's clearly been a modicum of success. But by and large there's been a kind of ghettoization of the discussion, in the academy at least, between those who think it's really the end of the world, that in our time this is far and away the most morally serious of all topics and we have to immediately deal with it, and those who just think that it's one of many interesting but not necessarily immediately pressing topics. Those prone to apocalypticism are certainly to be applauded for their seriousness about proposing worked out, concrete alternatives, and the other side does remind us that this is not the only issue for Christians to worry about. But the polarization of the discussion is unfortunate and counterproductive because it tends to obscure the ways in which environmental concerns can't really be addressed piecemeal, because they impinge on the way we do most things in the modern world. So ironically, both sides are right: concern for the environment is a core and pressing issue, but one that ought to bring Christians to think about all other issues in a different configuration, in ways I touched on at the end of the previous interview.[1]

A broader failure of most academic and practical ethics, and here I mean targeted ethics courses like business ethics or medical ethics, is that they simply don't deal with the topic at all. Business ethics as a discipline tends to focus on not cheating on your taxes, telling the truth, keeping your contracts, those sorts of topics, and in this it is typical of all the more practice-based strains of ethical discussion. In those discussions environmental questions simply have no way to emerge. This takes me back to something I've touched on several times now, that the place we must begin to think is not by debating policy solutions for today's environmental issues. We never really encounter environmental ethics as a discrete dilemma because "the environment" is not a discrete ethical topic, a topic that we can think

1. See chapter 5.

about on its own. To think of it as a discrete topic entails a methodological decision about what ethics is. If we make "the environment" an ethical problem that needs to be solved, the problem is so big, and touches on so many things, that for most people the simple scale of the problem means that it will be deferred for later discussion, simply because we've narrated the theme in such a way that no one of us can really get a handle on it or respond to it in a meaningful way. Instead of framing as you have in your question ("where has Christian higher education has failed to address environmental ethics?"), I would prefer to talk about how our ways of framing the issue are a core part of the problem. The failure is our thinking of "the environmental crisis" as a discrete topic rather than as a sort of screen or report card on which the cumulative effects of our lifestyles is projected.

I would prefer to ask how the game changes if we think of Christian ethics as characterized by an "ethos of attention to creaturely context" or something along those lines. Such an approach could take environmental concerns very seriously but would integrate these concerns in a much deeper and methodologically serious way with the problem of living in illusions and the lack of perceptual sensitivity that would link with all ethical discussions that are typically seen as very remote from environmental concerns. That's at least a starting point.

How in your own specific circumstances have you chosen to utilize the role of a lecturer in a prominently recognized school of divinity within a larger secular university to take on board this challenge? How would you specifically approach that issue in the context of your own work?

I have long been involved, and hope to be more involved in the future, with cross-disciplinary university discussions of all sorts of relevant practical questions, around renewable energies, for instance, or energy use and mobility. Ongoing discussions in various sectors of the university are relevant to theologians, and often there is some very interested and sophisticated thought going on in these contexts from which theologians can learn a lot.

There are also higher-level theoretical questions that are useful to engage. Our leading anthropologist, Tim Ingold, is also thinking about many of the themes I have discussed in these interviews. He is very thoughtful about energy, observing for instance that animals have for millennia been the main energy source augmenting human work. Animals and slaves have been the main ways humans have trapped and utilized energy beyond our own physical strength in order to boost our ability to get work done, in addition to photosynthesis. Water, wind, and steam power came only recently, not to mention the power extracted from oil, which we now think of as the baseline source of energy. Those sorts of discussions can become very fruitful because they help us as Christians read Scripture in more interesting ways and give us fresh angles from which we might begin to see the biblical place of energy. The Bible, after all, is a book begun and finished during the period in which slaves and animals were the only available sources to do the jobs we understand "energy" to be doing for us now. Such fresh angles into Scripture can only mean that Christians gain a sharper view of how the same God who was working in biblical times is working now.

Let me back up and make one terminological point: I don't tend to use the language of "the environment" at all. In theological terms, the environment of human life is divine activity. Salvation history is the determinative environment of human life. From this perspective we can see how the contemporary language of "the environment" imports a mechanistic picture in which the ebb and flow of the material world is taken to be our "real" environment. This way of understanding "the environment" thinks of earth like a space capsule packed with finite resources that must be utilized like we're on a life raft. The ethical implications of dropping one definition for the other is important because each sets up such different frames of reference or moral equations within which we can ask questions about what it means to be responsible creatures. We get a very different picture from the lifeboat account if we begin by affirming in faith that all of creation is created good as a forum for the reciprocal relations of creatures and for their flourishing. Such a question foregrounds the ethical task of finding our appropriate place within a good and plentiful creation, in contrast to the demand that we figure out how to hang on to every last molecule of resource for future generations. We can be confident in faith in the goodness and benevolence of the Creator within one picture, while within the other we cannot help but give fear a central role in our ethical thinking.

This is, for me, an absolutely fundamental issue: How can we think seriously about so-called "environmental questions" in a faith and hope that will allow our action to be confident and assured rather than succumbing to the fear of catastrophe that for very obvious reasons is so tempting? Christ did not die so that we could live in fear. And it is again pointing to the conceptual and existential primacy of the environment of divine working when the psalmist says "the fear of the Lord is the beginning of wisdom." We don't have to fear environmental apocalypse. But we do well to ask what the Ruler and Judge of our lives makes of the ways in which we treat the works of God's hands.

Such big-picture-framing moves make a lot of difference down close to the ground. For instance, I sit on an Equality and Diversity Committee at the university, and we recently had a revealing conversation about how to incentivize people to drive less. This committee is concerned with making sure that the university is an environment in which women and minorities and disabled people get a fair shake, systemically. The vice principal, who chairs the committee, is a lawyer and very interested in equality and diversity issues but for ecological reasons also very much wants to set up incentives and disincentives so university employees drive less often to campus. To this end he was pushing to raise university parking charges. That position sparked a discussion about what such a policy might do to mothers who have children in school at various places or disabled people, both of whom, given how our cities are arranged, can't really survive without driving.

This raises the more fundamental issue of how a basic ecological sensibility must be enacted within the social fabric of a specific place as it exists, with its ability, or lack of ability, to carry the more vulnerable or more threatened members of our community. It is those concrete, practical skirmishes in which the meanings of these broad theoretical frameworks ultimately get hammered out, sharpened, and clarified. Yes, for ecological reasons we want to disincentivize driving, but not in a way that places further hurdles in the way of the more vulnerable, given the current structures of our society.

Your example is a sensitive one. St. Andrews has taken a carrot-and-stick approach. It is made clear to everyone admitted to the university that the university has an ecological commitment that discourages the use of private automobiles. A brief explanation of the reasons for this position is included. Then they go on to say, "And, as a consequence, we recognize a responsibility to offer a quality of life which is not impeded by the absence of a private automobile." The university has committed to providing a stock of perimeter university housing so that students can live within walking distance of all the university's major resources.

They recently, for example, sold property that had been gifted to the university that was relatively close to the center of town. Nevertheless,

because it was in an outlying village, at least a quarter-of-an-hour away by bus, they sold the gifted property in order to ensure that resources are available to purchase more property that is immediately adjacent to the university, whenever it comes on the market. The university has committed to a town-and-gown environment that is supportive of both the community and the students, and the local community is also very committed to this premise. They don't want to be turned into a large pedestrian mall. They've made that clear. But nevertheless, they appreciate that insofar as this is possible, students ought not monopolize large segments of the town that needs still to have space for people to live who are retired, families, visitors. So there's been a very constructive dialogue around the issue of mobility. Thus far I have been very impressed that the university has made substantive economic decisions to back that up.

That's exactly the sort of commitment to political consensus and sustainable cites that I would like to see more of, and I haven't picked up the positive side of that commitment being as clearly articulated at the University of Aberdeen. The furthest we've gotten is "we'll put on a special shuttle from the medical campus to the main campus," which has not been working very well. But there do seem to be a few people who are at least aware that setting up more bus routes between discrete parts of the university and penalizing all other available ways to get to and around campus is disadvantaging those who are already pushing uphill in our cities. It is very easy for these sorts of piecemeal reformulations of mobility to really make students' lives harder.

You've cited a nicely concrete environmental policy that ties together your various interests: education, universities, and ecological sensitivity. The beauty of your example is that in addition to being a more sustainable arrangement in terms of energy use, it also takes into account the ecologies of the student experience, the ecology of the city aside from students, and almost certainly the ecology of the green space around the city, an aspect of discouraging urban sprawl. If we want students to come to lectures, the majority of whom are able to walk, then it's a no-brainer to set up our cities presuming that they will use that entirely renewable resource that will at the same time wake them up a little bit! There's a whole eco-system being thought through here that is far more sustainable than one in which people are using vehicles of any kind, really. So that's the sort of direction that I would love to see all sorts of discussions moving.

Again, if I may refer to St. Andrews and ask you to comment by comparison with your own campus. The grounds adjacent to our immediate residential area border on something called Lade Braes, an ancient pathway going back to the period when this area of St. Andrews was part of the extensive grounds of a priory and monastery. Lade Braes traverses a series of botanic gardens and parks, a wide, scenic grassy area overgrown with meadows and arbors that runs the length of one entire section of the city and connects all the residential areas so that students and the general public and senior citizens and families with children have an alternative to walking next to the roads. The pathway was constructed using Roman methods, which begin by digging down six to eight feet, building up a water-permeable base with rock so water does not build up to freeze and crack the surface, which is then covered with soil and cobblestones. This cobbled surface is in turn covered with gravel for traction.

Earlier we touched on the theme of the wisdom of making foot travel corridors an integral part of a city, when we discussed the Dutch decision to organize new builds around cycling corridors.[2] I think that both arrangements are brilliant, for so many reasons.

Aberdeen, like most oil cities, aspires to achieve almost the opposite arrangement, or at least the high number of oil executives and workers strongly tend to prefer investing in a car-commuting-friendly infrastructure. But like most European cities, in the older parts of town infrastructural remnants of a foot-travel world remain, and those can be augmented or obliterated. Aberdeen University is in Old Aberdeen, which is a few miles from the port and was in fact separated from Aberdeen proper by a green belt up until the early modern era. The world really didn't ask much of us, meaning that there wasn't a lot of infrastructural change for a very long time. The result was that on a daily basis we still use many of the ancient footpaths around Old Aberdeen, which have been the cathedral and university sector of the region for 600 years now.

Old Aberdeen was never really more than a single high street, and up until the modern period, you were very happy to have a paved high street at all. If you did, that's where you wanted to walk. Everybody's house fronted the one road and was open to the fields behind because everyone kept some livestock. The modern city that subsequently built up around the old city built up gently enough that you can still go pretty directly on foot to most

2. See chapter 4.

places in Old Aberdeen and therefore around the campus, which is very compact by American standards, and is also, unlike most American campuses, thoroughly intermixed with non-university properties and private houses.

But Aberdeen is certainly not St. Andrews in that we have working heavy industry in the city, and the oil business has a very different ethos than what you get in an essentially university and (golf) tourist town. For heavy industry, the bigger the machines you can use to move things around the more efficient and economically productive everything becomes. Part of our port has been in continuous use for 700 years, but it has continually been expanded over the years as it served various purposes, and has now become the main supply port for the North Sea oil rigs. It is now a very busy port, and has several industrial-size bays that generate a lot of truck traffic going in and out, hence Aberdeen being awash with oil money from people who are working in the business and out on the rigs.

We can grasp how differently this configures discussions about city planning by returning to the debate about what to do about the big park in the middle of Aberdeen proper, which is about two miles away from Old Aberdeen. The old main part of Aberdeen proper is built on seven bridges over several substantial valleys, a remarkable feat of engineering that took place during the eighteenth and nineteenth centuries and established what is now the town's main street. This has left, however, one large valley uncovered right in the middle of town, in which the Victorians constructed a very nice sunken garden. As we discussed earlier, the wealthy local oilman Ian Wood wants to raise the gardens to street level, which would be a massive engineering project to span a substantial void that has a four-lane road and train tracks running through it, in addition to the park. One of the subtexts of discussions about whether or not to go ahead with development became apparent when people starting suggesting the possibility that if they can enclose such a big space there is potential for there to be a huge underground parking structure right in the middle of town.

The latest skirmish in the war has been the debates in city council meetings about whether or not it will hold a referendum on the development, and it now looks like the opponents of the project have won the day so that only residents of the city will be able to vote. The newspaper editors, who are partisans for the project, complained bitterly in print about this, because they know that without the votes of the people of the shire, who want to live outside Aberdeen and drive in to shop or work, the inhabitants of the city will vote the project down primarily because of the huge costs involved, but also because of the obviously narrow vision of what is to be gained by doing it. I've given you a bit more detail about this story just to convey the way that the equation in Aberdeen is very different from St. Andrews, and in many ways, it is probably more like the situation in most urban areas in the English-speaking developed world, in which razing the old and replacing it with something new is considered the essence of city improvement.

Here Germany seems interesting in that many German cities built up since the end of World War II strove to preserve both the strong commitment to the fabric of the community, but also to allow a car-culture. This has generated a series of urban studies that now have resulted in some very interesting urban policies, such as requiring all buildings to have green roofs. We're not talking here about patios with a few potted plants. They're talking about truly green roofs that are going to be used to offset a rising heat index due to the increased numbers of concrete buildings, paved roads, and the loss of green space. Joint studies are ongoing with the city of Chicago, which has initiated a similar plan. Because Chicago has a multitude of multi-story skyscrapers, turning entire roofs into massive outdoor parks means that people might not even realize they are over a multi-level parking structure.

These are examples of urban studies in major urban contexts both on the continent and in North America that grapple with these issues and at the same time try to avoid core death, the concentration of businesses which close after five or seven o'clock in the evening. When cities entirely shut down for long portions of the day they attract crime and all sorts of problems. Chicago now mandates that, depending on the size of the building, the upper quarter or third of every high-rise complex must be residential. At the same time they've also mandated the use of what are called "sky-bridges" that link buildings in order to generate something like a series of floating villages in which restaurants and a wide variety of entertainment and leisure-pursuit facilities and churches are connected and accessible by foot. Below there is a business sub-strata, and at the ground level, the pedestrian level, they have prohibited buildings having large unbroken expanses of glass that are dark at night. You must integrate access and theatre facilities and restaurants so that you maintain a viable core life for the city.

It seems to me that this is an area in which Christians, who have for some time been people both of the country and of the city, can engage in serious and perhaps unique ways. Might you have any thoughts regarding the Christian view of the city in terms of Christian tradition and its place in history, environmentally speaking?

Let me add one footnote to your comparison of Chicago and Germany. What I was calling an environmental ethos is simply more obvious amongst the Germans. The Jewish philosopher Theodor Adorno, while displaced to America from Germany during the Second World War, wrote in *Minima Moralia* that he was struck by how the roads through the American deserts of the West made him feel that no one had ever run their hands in love through the hair of this land.[3] Americans just drive a road straight through the land as the bird flies. There are of course similar direct road and rail corridors in Germany, but the overall land use in the country is very different from America. The country as a whole has a strikingly high population density, but it's not in big cities. It's in towns and small villages. This is why they have both an interest in there being cars, but also in not ending up with the same kinds of congestion that you get in American cities. But they've put their cities and manufacturing industry together in very different ways to meet this challenge, starting with the presumption that the older ways of letting the land define how space will be used are to be respected rather than erased in the name of progress. Perhaps because their cities were bombed to oblivion, they recognize that older buildings were built to last, to be cared for, and are therefore resistant to the prefabricated architecture that is so dominant in North America that is not designed to last, and is therefore very hard to care for. In my view these are some of the differences that emerge when you take environmental questions to be an add-on concern verses an ecologically sensitive ethos that becomes a subtext of all thinking about building and living in places.

Having lived in Germany for nearly two years, and having visited many times, I still find it difficult to recall seeing any parking structures at all, garden-topped or not. How do they manage that? You certainly can't go to any big American city and miss the multi-story parking garages. So there are some tricks of infrastructural arrangement that are embedded in German cities that I think would bear further thought from an American perspective.

---

3. Adorno, *Minima Moralia*, 48.

Now to your question about Christianity and the city. It's an old chestnut, the city versus the rural life debate, one that rumbles on in various ways in our aesthetic sense about the beauty of the countryside in contrast to the ugliness of cities, and our political discussions, in which cities are far and away taken to be places where excitement and culture are to be had. Jacques Ellul's *The Meaning of the City* is the best theological treatment of the topic that I know. I'm sure that he's right that the city is depicted in the Fall narratives as one of the effects of the Fall, and in the eschatological narratives it's also part of where humanity is going. Some of the pivotal moments in the Old Testament take place in rural settings and almost all the New Testament takes place in urban settings. In my view the overall yield of these very brief observations is the assertion that Christianity is neither an urban nor a rural religion, and a fully-developed Christian theology will have something to say about both of these scenes of human life and their interrelations.

I find your account of the city-country relation in Scripture very interesting. Yet there are also those who insist that in Scripture the cities have a very special role to play, which is made somewhat more problematic because they are often the seats of power. One can think of the importance rebuilding Jerusalem took on as an Old Testament concern, how rebuilding the walls became a symbol of place for the Jewish people, especially after the Babylonian captivity. Today, of course, it would be something of a political understatement to say that Jerusalem has a critical role to play in the sense of place of both Palestinians and the Jewish people.

But as a Christian would you be willing to comment on whether Christians should become more engaged, for example, in city planning, in academic higher education, or in medical boards of review? Are there ways in which a constructive beginning could be at the level of higher education that might offer a sort of prototype for future integrative professional thinking?

I can definitely speak to that. I've discussed in writing an idea that I learned from Wendell Berry, that one starting point is to notice how the relationship between rural and urban is not that of producer and consumer.[4] I think that's the standard subconscious late-modern assumption about the relationship. Farmers are confined to the cultural wilderness in order to

4. See Brock, *Christian Ethics in a Technological Age*, 358.

grow food and all of the interesting things are happening in the city where none of us have to prepare our food, we only consume. I tried to work a bit in the technology book to show how that picture mischaracterizes both sides of the equation because in the most basic sense none of us is capable of producing the things that matter in sustaining human life, for all the reasons we talked about in the last interview. We receive the things that matter, and this is especially obvious in the realm of agriculture. The rejection of this polarity also resists thinking of the home as the place where we live our private lives of consumption after we have gone to work to produce things. That polarity is a theological misdescription of what it means to live our lives. Ideally I would like to see Christians not only doing without a production-consumption polarity, but I'd like them to give up the language of human production entirely. We can do some pretty amazing things, but because we are not gods or the Creator, we will always be hunters, gatherers, and tinkerers, and when we start putting on airs about being producers and creators, which usually goes with raptures at how imaginative we are, trouble is sure to follow.

Think about education, for instance. We simply misunderstand it if we approach it as a commodity to be produced and sold so we can go and buy the things we want. It is itself a vocation tied to the fertility of human life, namely, training doctors and lawyers and engineers who care for constituencies, parts of the political fabric, the health of the people, the peace of the people, the hard structures in which they live their lives. The university was initially conceived and for a long time was devoted to training two professions in particular, doctors and lawyers, along with the pastors of the church. The educational institution was thus organized to serve the welfare of all people by training those three vocations chosen very intentionally and for theological reasons that we discussed in the last hour—to sustain the *ecclesia*, *politia*, and *oeconomia*. That's why universities sprang from the church—the church had a theological interest in serving the stability and strength of the institutional forms of medicine, law, and the church, because these were taken to serve and support the basic human activities any society needs to survive. At this time, of course, they assumed that the guilds would take care of educating craftsmen and builders, and farmers and those caring for animals would learn from their parents. But in theological terms, everyone was being trained to find their place in serving the provisioning and care of the whole people.

The university in that sense was also neither a producer nor a consumer but a place where knowledge of how to care for things is passed on. And in that very specific sense it is doing the same thing that the farmer is doing, passing on knowledge of animal husbandry or agricultural practice about what it means to live as creatures and to receive God's care for creatures. I find it significant to teach theology in a building in which theology has been taught for hundreds of years, and to begin every day with prayer in the chapel at the heart of the university that was used for prayer each day hundreds of years ago by the monks who first taught here. The buildings are reminders in stone and wood of what I've been trying to say about the role of education as a whole: our task is to receive the wisdom about life in this world that is carried in traditions, not to immediately assume that we can do things better.

To continue an earlier example, I think German Christians have been asking such questions for a long time, even though in one infamous period this interest in Mother Earth and being close to Mother Earth overwhelmed other crucial theological priorities. Nevertheless, that sense that Christianity is something that strives to make life livable in specific places and takes the lives that have been lived before in those places as teachers to be respected is often drowned out by the Christianity that aims to save souls by getting people to heaven while believing in this life in the economics of creative destruction and planned obsolescence and the benevolence of the invisible hand of free markets.

Having touched upon how the critical paradigm shift out of the producer-consumer polarity has economic implications, could you explore with us how you might want to see Christian higher education succeeding in its engagement with economic studies?

A nice place to start would be for Christians to stop modeling themselves on executive business models. Most pastors in megachurches during the last twenty years have MBAs, not theology degrees, and as we speak many small Christian colleges are being converted into a for-profit model that is very much producer-consumer oriented.[5] Many megachurches now construct their campuses on a business office model, and come up with corporate management titles like "executive pastor." It's pretty obvious there is a

---

5. See the PBS Frontline documentary, "College Inc.," first broadcast 4 May 2010 and accessible online.

marked shift in theological presuppositions behind these sociological facts, one in which effectiveness and success are defined in very specific ways. You're looking to get people in the pews, saved, and baptized and tithing to support the brand and the budget so you can move on to the next field ripe for harvest and set up a church plant. Or you're seeing the market in "Christian higher education" as ripe for the picking, and you're asking private investors to float you the cash so that you can get the operation running and generate a cash flow to investors. If that's your account of Christianity then those secular disciplines that promise productivity in those terms are going to be very attractive and may well lead to performance gains judged on this scale. I think that's what we're seeing all around us. I would be very pleased to see the language of leadership drop entirely out of Christian discourse as well as executive management models, and I hope I'm not the only one who finds the language of "executive pastor" physically nauseating. That we can make church what it needs to be by being better managers is, I think, a very widespread and destructive trend in contemporary, especially Protestant, Christianity. Those are places where I think an alternative witness is both extremely important and difficult.

And how would you like to see those conceptions replaced?

Let's think about a strand of that position that is popular at the moment, the argument for culture-making James Hunter makes in *To Change the World*. He begins: if Christians are doing what they ought to be, they will be changing the culture. And that means they need to be good at whatever it is that they're doing, good enough in their fields to become cultural leaders. They need to be successful, in worldly terms, in whatever discipline they are pursuing, engineering, music composition, novel writing, whatever. While he's certainly talking about engagement in the world, for theological reasons I'd like to see it described very differently.

What I would like to see is a far more fine-grained interest in the problems of specific places, and the qualities of specific places, and the values of specific things, and more to the point, I would like to hear an explanation of what sort of things Christians might also be about that could in some situations counterbalance their desire to be the best doctor or lawyer described in purely technical terms. Here again I have the concern about Christians getting sucked into self-absorption and worldly standards of performance. There's certainly nothing in the book about being world-class foster parents or top-notch carers for a dying family member, or for being a great stay-at-home mom or a nurse who is always behind because he attends to patient needs that are not recognized by the priorities of a hospital. That's not culture changing in Hunter's opinion, and this gap in his treatment ought to have been more obvious than it seems to have been to his many fans.

If you are committed to Chicago, to return to that discussion, and committed to the people of Chicago, you will see that the parameters of the lives being lived in many parts of that city and the infrastructure in which those lives are lived out are all wrong. Christians should be the ones caring about those things and therefore involved in discussions of urban planning or architecture. And there are times at which caring in this way may be interesting but counterproductive if judged in terms of advancing one's professional success. Here I would suggest that William Stringfellow's witness as a lawyer in Harlem in the late 1960s,[6] or Jean Vanier's living with disabled people outside Paris,[7] are clear witnesses to another vision of Christianity. Even banking can be approached as a vocation that aims to empower people rather than make money. The micro-lending and community farming[8] movements are wonderful attempts to ask how we can really make people's lives better in a concrete way by paying more attention to the lives being lived right next door. But all these movements depend on something I've stressed several times before, a renewal of perception, and they require a sharper empirical eye. I'll put it this way: in my experience, at least in North America, there are far more Christians who will drive through a main street and notice, "Oh, look, a new restaurant that has come in that is kind of new and trendy, I would like to go there," than will notice the types of infrastructure issues that we're talking about or even the signs of embedded social distress that signal the need for people to pay more attention and care.

To speak biographically, I grew up in an oil town. Its oldest part is only about seventy years old, and there the houses were shotgun style, prefab-type houses built right next to the refinery gate. As people made more money they started building homes farther away from the plant, out in the country, with much of the city coming to be strung out in awkward clusters along a pair of roads that just led north into at that time empty country. The town became quite spread out, and when it was eventually incorporated

6. Stringfellow, *My People Is the Enemy.*
7. His story appears in Spink, *The Miracle, the Message, the Story.*
8. Brown, "When the Uprooted Put Down Roots."

three different little hamlets were pulled in to form one big three-cornered town with a refinery in the middle of it. This town was guaranteed to force you to drive a lot. Meanwhile, the oldest parts of the town were being progressively left behind.

Over the years the wages for heavy industrial work had been steadily rising, and all those workers wanted new houses in the subdivisions, which then sprang up in random constellations. At some point all the business-citing logarithms by which America is built these days began to register that there was enough cash flow in this little town to warrant some investments. But when one of these triggers is pulled, they all fire at the same time. If the logarithms say that there's enough wealth in the city to warrant a Target then you'll also get a K-Mart. Next to them will come twinned eateries, a Pizza Hut and a Chick-fil-A and with them an "upscale" pair of sit-down restaurants, a Chili's and an Olive Garden. All this happens automatically because the decisions about where chain businesses will be built are primarily dictated by a logarithm that looks at densities of population and financial flow. When the numbers hit a certain threshold then all of the computers say that at this place it is time to build, because there's money to be made. And of course none of the chains want to be left out.

The effects have been quite obvious along the twinned main street in my hometown, which now is one long parade of hastily thrown up chain-store barns surrounded by massive parking lots. The ones that were built after I'd already left fifteen years ago are now already empty or filled with cut-rate sorts of "here's a space and let's figure out what to do with it" businesses, while the progression of ever larger metal-hangar superstores marches toward the highway to the north up the town's parallel roads, replacing the green field land where before Longhorn steers grazed with pavement and generous sodium lighting. There was never any awareness that green space meant anything more than "potential development," and here land was unzoned and cheap buildings designed to last ten years could be built and left behind at an astonishing rate.

Houston has no city planning law, so there's not even any zoning. And the town that I grew up in was part of that larger landscape. Absolute, unfettered capitalism was thus the law that ordered building in what is by any account a highly Christianized region. So I've traveled the road myself out of a Christian-shaped deafness and active resistance to even asking the sorts of questions that we're discussing. I think it's probably not unrelated that there was a ten-square-mile refinery at the heart of that triangular city.

You can't live around that part of the energy business without taking a certain view of what energy means. That's a long answer that perhaps gives you more of a sense as to why I think asking the questions you're asking are really quite critical.

Could I ask you to address an issue that is growing in prominence within many evangelical circles here in Britain? The idea of this being the end times is being promoted by a number of evangelical parachurch organizations that are widely respected and influential in many denominations in the United States. Some would say that we are not that far away from views held by medieval Christians, when life expectancy was about thirty-four for vast portions of the population and the focus was very much on the afterlife. The evangelical community has appropriated a theology that says Christ is coming soon and therefore our focus needs to be on numbers. This explains, for example, why they would focus on building large, simple warehouse-like churches with a very dynamic ministry of outreach, and have a sense that one should not be too engaged with the environment because it will distract you from the real purpose of the Christian faith.

Theologically it's important to hold on to both sides of the equation. Luther said that since the end is near we should be planting apple trees, and he certainly thought the end times were upon him. If the end is near, then there is something at stake in how we live today, and this is good. This eschatological tension is appropriately a motor for Christian action, and has been expressed in all sorts of ways in the Christian tradition. Augustine, for instance, was arguably an activist, intervening in imperial governance and writing letters on all sorts of issues all the time. But he thought about Christ's coming all the time. He yearned to be over the horizon of time, but he believed that this yearning to be outside of time allowed him to relate appropriately to the things of this world.

So both Augustine and Luther thought that the end of time was pressing in on their lived lives, but neither of them thought this was any warrant not to invest wholly in this world. Quite the reverse. This suggests that the "lifeboat's sinking" account of what it means that Christ's return is imminent is a withered version of traditional views, and has replaced them with another eschatology in which we can trash this place because we're about to get picked up. This sounds more like the co-option of the Christian story of the end in order to defend a vision of aggressive capitalism than it does any form of traditional Christianity, and it would also suggest why there is a convergence between conservative Christians' attraction to certain forms of accelerated capitalism and the booming business in end-times fiction.

At Pentecost Christians are taught that the *eschaton* is not just "later." What Jesus inaugurates and the Spirit continues is a heavenly kingdom that arrives now. Eternal life has in some sense begun in this time, in creation as we know it, and in this kingdom people live in a different way. A core image in Revelation is the heavenly city coming down to earth (Rev 21). In the New Testament heaven refuses to stay "up there." It makes its presence palpable here and now. In the kingdom of Heaven we are restored to live as the creatures we were created to be, as those who can tend and care for a garden, our place, and do so in attentiveness to what God's word tells us about that place, but also how that place makes its own demands on our care.[9] In a properly Christian theology the beginning and end are fulfilled in the middle, in Jesus Christ. It is therefore wrong to oppose this-worldliness and other-worldliness.

How, then, ought we to take the Letter to the Romans, which speaks of all creation being subject to the consequences of the Fall, so that it too can be resurrected into the glory of the Children of God, which is echoed in much Catholic and Orthodox systematic approaches to the issue you've highlighted? Would Christ's resurrection, in tandem with Pentecost, be the actual beginning of the restored world that is in process now, or will it not appear until the second coming? Those would seem to be two very different readings than the theology of evangelical groups, who might lean toward an ahistorical approach.

Though Catholic and Orthodox positions are quite different in their internal framing of the matter, I would agree with them that the earth is renewed by Christ making human beings into his image, and that this remaking is not just of their souls, but of their whole lives and bodies. If we agree with them on this we are left with the shocking implications that a lot of evangelical theology is basically deist. It operates as if the essence of the church does not penetrate all the way down into earthiness, materiality. We live in a fallen world, and the earth will keep on groaning until it is swallowed up in the conflagration of the end times, but we can have our hearts changed,

9. See Brock, "Creation: Mission as Gardening."

we can be nicer to each other, and we can be saved from hellfire and go to heaven. There are a handful of crucial theological claims that ground an account of salvation that is so other-worldly, and many of those have precursors in the tradition, but the fact remains that evangelicals, by and large, seem attracted to a picture of the relation of time to eternity that slides far too easily into an "it'll all be over soon" ethic. I take this to be much too socially conservative in addition to being a theologically thin account of Christ's living salvific activity.

7

Medicine, Daily Bread, Politics, and Violence

Please speak to the role of a Christian facilitator confronting environmental ethical dilemmas in a secular society. Could you explore some instances where the rubber meets the road in your role as an author, Christian participant in secular organizations, or in academic contexts where the secular and Christian perspectives are actively confrontational and benefit from the Christian facilitator's role?

If I am hearing you right, your question imagines discussions that might take place as something like a public debate. I think we've covered in previous interviews why that really doesn't feel like the main forum in which I do my work, so I'll begin from the conceptual end and say what I think I'm doing in the forums in which I would be facing more confrontational discussions.

Also, though I do get into confrontations now and then, I like to flank them by doing the harder work of trying to display why there may be other options besides the commonsense and usual ways of framing what counts as a dilemma. Call this "soft" confrontation by redirection!

Earlier we spoke about energy demand and the likelihood that energy costs will be going up and how that creates pressures to find ways to protect our supply. We are often presented with the dilemma of "securing our energy future" or "finding new energy sources," basic questions that will sharply determine what counts as a good answer. Many if not most of our ethical discussions could be so much more fruitful if we just recognized the ways in which we constrict the discussion, sometimes intentionally, by asking the wrong questions. So I've typically understood my role to be attempting to explain why we should try to back up one step and ask, "What, really, is the dilemma?" I often do that by trying to tease out the ways in which our habits as Westerners approaching various issues are both describable and limiting. Let's start with the example of medicine, which has been on both of our minds lately.

Western medicine, as highly sophisticated and successful as it is, still has fairly sharp boundaries around its imagination as to what counts as treatment. If we boil down to the bare minimum the way in which Western medicine conceives treatment, its main modalities are ultimately only killing, deadening, or excising, not different in kind from the medicine that has been practiced in the West since the days of leeches and surgery without anesthetic. It's not accidental that we use terms like "invasive surgery." Our core metaphors for medical care are ones that assume that if we can cut out the problem, kill it, or deaden it, then the problem is solved. Philosophically the same assumptions guide developments in surgery, psychotropic drugs, chemotherapy, and transplantation. If we are trying to get a sense of how Western society goes about confronting the challenges to its living, and its habitual resort to certain kinds of solutions, this is a worthwhile first point of call, though I regret that I'll have to leave aside discussion of attempts to create genetic therapies, which represent a bit of a twist but not really an overturning of this paradigm, and regenerative medicine and current work with stem cells, which do suggest the beginning of a different paradigm peeking over the horizon.

This has been on my mind a lot lately again, dealing as we are with Adam's chemotherapy treatment regime. This week's evocative moment came during a discussion with several doctors and nurses about how to deal with pain he is having in his mouth. Chemo kills cells that replicate quickly and it therefore hits the mouth and digestive tract very hard. His mouth is all torn up with ulcers so he can't eat, and if he can't eat he gets dehydrated, and if he gets dehydrated he's put on a saline drip, which is obviously quite a mechanical, invasive intervention—to stick a needle in someone's vein and fill them up with fluid—that we'd like to avoid, because it is never fun to keep up with an eight-year-old tethered to a fluid pump for four hours by a needle in his arm.

There are much more low-level, hands-on ways to decrease pain, to receive and augment the given powers of recovery that a patient has. So simple mouth care—putting a warm cloth on somebody's mouth, working to try to find out things that are easy to eat that makes their mouth feel better and rehydrates the patient—simply doesn't count as treatment in modern hospital medicine. What really counts is a mouth spray that deadens the pain and that can be patented so that somebody can get a scientific paper and a promotion. James Hunter would call this "changing the culture," as we discussed in the last hour. I'm drawing out this example in order to use medicine as a lens that reveals how we as a society have deeply ingrained instincts about how to deal with problems that confront us. We're very good at killing and cutting and suppressing. But it's not necessarily our first instinct to ask how we might align ourselves with the healing capacities that God has already given.

You're drawing a distinction between a cultural perspective that reaches for modalities of killing or deadening or destroying as opposed to what might be an alternative approach, which envisages reinvigorating natural defenses within the body or enhancing metabolic capabilities including immune systems for healing.

I've drawn on this story because it's simply historically and sociologically a fact that other cultures have developed other sorts of medicines, though it's also indisputable that these other sorts of medicines haven't learned how to treat cancer. Even though they haven't, this doesn't mean Chinese medicine or other non-Western medicines weren't on to something, and the something that they were onto probably is not related to medicine, but to diet and lifestyle, so that fewer of them actually contract cancer. We know that cancer is a failure of the body's ability to suppress the uncontrolled replication of cells, which the body normally does. So yes, we can certainly throw a lot of effort into killing something that has gotten out of control because our weakened immune systems could not fight it off, but it is also worth considering what is right about a type of medicine that seems effectively to augment the forces of life that allow the body to keep cancerous processes at bay. Philosophically the approaches are remarkably different, which explains the outcry from doctors whenever "alternative medicines" seem to be gaining a foothold in medical schools or amongst the general populace. The reason such a contrast is interesting to me is that I think that the story

I'm telling about medicine is typical of the way Westerners construe problems and pose answers.

My overarching aim is to move from a theological perspective to help us all notice and recognize the many ways in which we rely on what we can't create. We can't really feed ourselves out of inanimate materials alone, we cannot manufacture food from things we've mined out of the ground—food has to be grown somehow. We can't really control weather, which means we can't control many aspects of the processes of food coming into being. If we try to control the weather, perhaps by building giant greenhouses, we do this at a high energy cost. We also can't produce healing. Nor can we produce political consensus or peace in any meaningful sense. All of those things just seem to happen, but are the necessary condition for all our manipulations to take place. Facing the reality that all we can do is intervene in processes we did not create and that are far bigger and more complex than we grasp raises more theological questions about what really sustains human life on earth, and how human life is related to the whole of creation. These are deeply theological questions.

To extend the example in the direction of environmental questions, as in medicine, progress in modern agriculture is often measured by noting the greater precision with which unwanted creatures can be effectively killed. Pesticides are essential to modern monoculture farming. Though this agriculture is "successful" in terms, for instance, of making some foodstuffs cheap, it comes with a host of associated problems both ecological in the sense of land degradation but also in terms of energy use. Again the core problem is one of a narrow vision of agriculture dominating other views. Can we think in different terms; imagine other ways of feeding humanity? It helps if we at least notice that there have clearly been many, many ways that agriculture has been organized.

I remember being in a cocoa plantation in the Dominican Republic that had layers of canopies that had been planted in an intentional way. An orchard need not be organized on the model of a single species of fruit trees being planted in lines in a field surrounded by useless ground grass. In this case cocoa plants, which need shade, were crouched in the shade of banana trees. The effect is to multiply the fertility of this local land economy, the different layers of organisms reinforcing one another, and all bearing fruit that we, and other animals, can eat. But it takes a different type of agriculture and human input to sustain such an ecosystem, which means different distributions of human habitation in the landscape, and so on. But it's obvious that this is a far more sustainable arrangement than most western agriculture, because it will work just fine without a tractor. It doesn't need irrigation. It works with essentially indigenous flora and fauna to create a stable ecosystem that produces food.

In *The Omnivore's Dilemma*, Michael Pollan devotes a long section to engaging Joel Salatin, who calls himself a grass farmer because he holds that it's the grass that really sustains whole farm systems. Cows eat the grass, and the chickens eat the grubs out of the cow manure so that there are fewer flies on the cows. The chickens are eating what they want to eat, and at the same time helping the manure to break down, and all of it happens in a way that over time gives the grass more of what it needs to grow. The system is a stable one that actually enriches the earth over time. The fertility of the soil increases and all the organisms living on it become healthier in the process. It thus very efficiently receives the divine gift of our daily bread that Jesus taught us to ask for from God.

Indians are now facing the opposite dilemma with the introduction of new species of grain. They have been farming with indigenous grains that over the centuries have had a 75 percent rate of return but have the capacity to resist disease and are indigenous to the area and can survive drought. Western agribusinesses promised them better yields in exchange for turning in their traditional seed stock, but what they received in turn is killing their native species while at the same time being decimated by disease. So while they had this enormous initial harvest, ever after they must always buy seed because the seed they have been given literally violates what we have come to accept as the most basic dimension of biological flora and fauna, which is that seed produces seed after its own kind.

The multinational agricultural seed companies such as Monsanto, based in the US, have succeeded in lobbying for domestic and international legal regimes that protect their business interests. It's not illegal to clean your own seed for next year's crop, but it is legal to patent crops, and because Monsanto has cornered markets like soybeans with their genetically modified versions, they can set up a blacklisting framework that works because they can credibly threaten farmers not to sell them next year's seed if they are caught cleaning seed to prepare it for the next year. They have systematically run out everyone who used to make a living going from farm to farm with the machinery that can turn fruit into seed. It's crazy being unable to prepare one's own seed. Seed cleaners are even followed by private detectives, who take down the names of the farms they're going to and those farmers are then threatened by Monsanto with being blackballed so that they can't buy fertilizer or the product that they need. This has been chillingly documented in the film *Food Inc.* A regulatory and economic infrastructure has been set up that is essentially the opposite of the sustainable picture that I've been painting of the grass farmer and the cocoa farms.

As absurd as this way of doing things seems when we look at it this way, within the larger plausibility framework within which we're all embedded, it makes sense to do agriculture the way we do it. We would have to pay more money to do it another way, at least in the short term. But at the end of the day Monsanto can't produce soybeans or soybean plants out of a test tube. They can alter and they can patent and they can try to extract financial gains from the processes of agriculture that long predate them. But what they can't do is produce life, in the same way that a doctor can't produce life from inanimate objects. Even more to the point, no one can stop drought. To jump back to the medical example, you can put as much chemo into the body as you like, but you're still hostage to the body healing itself. Even transplanting human organs relies on the healing properties of one human being to step in and cooperate with a second body's powers of healing in order to save that second human being who has lost an aspect of their bodily powers of healing.

P. D. James meditates on this fundamental dependence in her futuristic novel *Children of Men*, which explored what might happen if for some reason all humans became infertile. As a thought experiment it fleshes out the ways our whole society relies on something we can't really control: conception. We can manipulate conception but we can't really get it in hand. It eludes us. We can't create from nothing—we delude ourselves if we think we create life when we bring together human gametes to form test-tube babies. That's simply not what is happening, biologically speaking. The world starts to look very different when we begin to lose the control over these creaturely processes that we thought we had firmly gotten under control, as countless stories of infertility daily remind us. These insights were very vivid in the Middle Ages when the plague was a continual reminder to the whole civilized world that health was not something over which we had control. Our loss of that sort of sensibility is no little part of why we have an environmental problem. We have a hard time believing that there are processes in creation that we can't get under control if we want to. This is why it is important to recollect in very concrete contexts the ways in which we still don't have control, and here the fact that we cannot create but can only find political consensus is a salutary reminder of how the whole creaturely realm depends on conditions it cannot create, but on which it is utterly dependent.

The idea of the commons is a Christian idea with very deep historical roots, and which ruled out any claims to own things like species. Only recently has the West decisively repudiated this tradition with US businesses leading the charge to reject this legacy of Christendom because there is a lot of money to be made if you can somehow find a way to extract charges from things that people once did for free, like drinking water or growing crops. It is remarkable that, legally speaking, the turning point was a US Supreme Court ruling that allowed it was legal to patent life, a whole species, in this case an oil-eating bacterium. The reasoning the Court gave was that, due to its being genetically altered, this bacterium could be considered a human creation, a human invention.[1] It is because such theological mistakes are so deep-seated and currently being written into law that I am so insistent that we can't create anything, only God can create. All we can do is find and tinker. These affirmations were absolutely undisputed among Christians up until the last hundred years or so. Having lost touch with this basic theological claim and forgetting that we are not the Creator, we become destroyers. This is why the question of what is sustainable is not one that can be reduced to simple consumer choices about whether or not I should buy a Prius. It goes right through almost every sphere of modern life, which is heavily reliant on industrialized food production.

So when you ask me how I confront environmental questions in our society, it is because I think God is about giving us our daily bread that my interest gravitates to the question of how God cares for creation. I want to make Christians more aware of the ways in which we are in fact thwarting that divine care. The Western agricultural trajectory is very obvious in this respect in that it aspires to take the fertility of the earth in hand and actually make it better. We want tomatoes that can grow in a desert! There's an obvious air of dissatisfaction about it—75 percent return isn't enough if we can get 90 percent. But this kind of thinking has to sideline important ecological issues. We're talking again about what counts as development

---

1. The case under discussion is *Diamond vs. Chakrabarti*, which the US Supreme Court decided in 1980.

and what counts as success, what counts as economic productivity. We're not just interested in feeding people but in keeping the GDP up.

In general, then, I see my role in public as being a provocateur for those sorts of alternative questions to have an airing. There are already people out there raising one or the other of these particular problems, both in medicine and agriculture, and they often get into the sort of public debates that are the focus of your question. But not as many are talking about the theological beliefs that might drive us to embrace such activism, and that make the conceptual links between the different fields of activism. Nor are many people devoted to seeking out the places in human endeavor today that still, tacitly or explicitly, are built on an appreciation that can never be done by the application of force. Unfortunately it might be better to say that one of the tragedies of our historical moment that the only people who are looking for and appreciating what cannot be created but happens spontaneously are those devoted to data-mining and cloud sourcing, who are becoming increasingly sophisticated at making money from the basal metabolism and free intellectual contributions that make up human society. The essence of the problem is revealed by their description of their investigation as a "mining."

Jean Vanier has become an icon in refusing the techniques of force in his living with disabled people. I've come to appreciate just as much people who care in similar ways within the institutions of our modern world—special school teachers. The good special school teacher knows very well that they have to seek out and build up what capacities their students have, who are not like average children who just soak up learning like a sponge. There's a lot of skill involved in such teaching, which utilizes many techniques that have a very different structure than the ones that organize the majority of schools that, for instance, can rely on grades as incentives and punishments as disincentives.

Teachers in special schools are the opposite of "miners" because they must seek out and serve the powers of human life and intellect within modern educational systems that are essentially geared up for industrialized models of the mass production of knowledge, and so also have to learn the political skills they need to fight for the space and funding to have sufficient time to care for these students. Such teachers clearly have to be more aware of how modern society works and no doubt all children would benefit if their approaches were more widely deployed. We need more Christians who both fight to defend such spaces of care and who have the eyes to see that these fights are going on in pockets of resistance in many places in our societies. I find that if you can point people to those places, and describe them well, people just want to listen. Even if they think belief in God is bonkers, they are much more willing to give you a hearing instead of argue with you, if your approach is generating fresh ways of seeing the problems that they also find illuminating.

My technology book was recently reviewed by Timothy Gorringe, who pressed me on the linkage that I just made between the life that we cannot produce and the peace between people that we also cannot produce.[2] He suggested that if we sit around and wait for God to sort us out, well, God help us. Look at how much political disarray we have in the Anglican Church. His question takes us again to the nub of the issue because, if you think about it, the core of the global ecological crisis is the problem of political consensus. If the will were there to find a way to respond together to what we're doing to change the climate then it would be a fairly straightforward procedure for everybody to work in concert. But it is clear that we're shockingly far from any such political consensus.

All the problems that I've been raising are illuminated when we admit how difficult we find it to notice the ways we rely on the biological world. And political consensus is also something on which we're very reliant because if we can't agree about a common course of action and if we come to the point that we can't even agree if we're a "we" or just an agglomeration of antagonistic interest groupings, then our various governments will just sit in a stalled position as they essentially are now on environmental issues and nothing is going to happen.

Given this problem some philosophers, like Hans Jonas in *The Imperative of Responsibility*, therefore conclude: we're kind of in a lifeboat here. If we can't get our act together we'll have to bite the bullet and come up with a totalitarian world government that can force the issue. It will by now be clear that I have theological reasons to think that's altogether the wrong approach, and those reasons are of a piece with my criticisms of Western habits of dealing with the other problems we've been talking about. Politically speaking, totalitarian quashing of dissenting voices is equivalent to killing off plants you designate as weeds so that what you designate as fruit product can grow. You can do that in a very heavy-handed way by spraying to kill everything except the plant you want to grow. I refer to that as a mechanistic and manipulative solution. The same logic grounds the

2. Gorringe, "Review of *Christian Ethics in a Technological Age*."

Christian attraction to democratic rather than totalitarian governance. The political peace and agreement we need can never be reached by killing off dissent, but only by the power of speech to draw people together around a collective agreement.

Agricultural practice again exposes the essential ethical question. In Britain, in order to roll out proper industrialized, pesticide, petroleum and fertilizer monoculture, you're going to have to remove the hedgerows that once protected the fields from wind and controlled the movements of livestock. With the hedgerows go all the songbirds and the smaller animals that keep agricultural fertility up by eating the pests. There are always casualties when manipulative solutions are applied to any given problem. A totalitarian world government seems pretty obviously to me to be the manipulative solution applied to the political problem of finding consensus, and the fact that one of Germany's foremost contemporary public intellectuals (e.g., Jonas) is attracted to it, tells us that the problem of ethos reformation we are facing is a deep one.

We are not in a situation that we can force to a happy conclusion. We're in a position that is unsatisfactory for lots of reasons, not least because species are being killed off, rising sea levels threaten to inundate huge populations, droughts and extreme weather events seem to be increasing, and so on. We're in this situation and we can keep responding to it in the way that the last 200 years have taught us to deal with things, by trying to apply more force. The only alternative is some sort of paradigm shift, and I'm hoping that shift is generated at least in part by Christians relearning what it means to confess that God cares about us enough to have placed us in a world through which he is certainly able to feed us.

To reiterate, the traditional account of the three estates is an important aspect of my way into a theological recovery of receptivity. God has instituted the *ecclesia* as an institution in which God brings humanity into knowledge of God's self. The word *oeconomia* expresses God's concern—through both the processes of the natural world and the various institutions of human society—with the reproduction and feeding of human life. *Politia* names God's concern that humans live together in political peace, and his concern to uphold the institutions of human life that support it. In each of these three realms theological thought offers us incisive views of the things God has tended to care about, and of the ways he cares for humans even when they rebel against him. It is a theological concept that offers theologians a critical angle from which to raise questions about what we're taking for granted, and what we think we can get under control.

So when, for instance, the government starts to think about its populace as a resource, like a natural resource, theologians have a vantage point from which to respond, "That's really a confusion of categories. The purpose of government is not to treat human populations as natural resources that need to be used or maximized or 'mined' to achieve some other end." Because God cares for every human being our societies need to be arranged in ways that recognize the worth of each human life. God is interested in fostering societies that do just that, not governments that see their own citizens as resources, some being better off dead, or better off never having come into existence, or as too expensive to maintain.

Could I ask you continue exploring for us this very interesting analogy you've introduced? Increasingly in the West we have come to rely on the notion of military presence; for example, discussions of nuclear and biological warfare tend to assume that peace can be achieved through threats to destroy.

You've hit on another deep, structuring insight as to how I think all of this hangs together. Ultimately, the way the developed world intervenes in the processes of life is violent. So it shouldn't be any surprise that at the far edge of our ways of gaining control are tanks and machine guns. It shouldn't surprise us that the bedrock on which our society rests is this violence.

I wouldn't be able to offer a fine-grained account of the stages of the relevant cultural development, but it does seem pretty obvious to me that the rise of the spin doctor is an indicator that the attempt to manage every aspect of reality that we see in the biological realm is playing out in a very similar manner in the political realm. Rather than talking regularly and at length with their constituents, politicians chart their course by more controlled approaches, looking at focus groups or economic indicators of behavior in order to come to conclusions about what constituents think. The old definition of representative government as listening and then following the expressed will of the people is replaced with a model in which we don't really need to ask people what they want us to do because we can track how people are voting with their pocketbooks. The assumption is that we know what the electorate wants from us as politicians because we have real-time feedback mechanisms that are different in kind from the feedback mechanism that is the town hall meeting where you ask people what they think. Politics has become a matter of keeping tabs on the ebb and flow of those opinions that make it into the press and which an expert called "the spin doctor" keeps under control, having been trained to ensure that expressed public opinions do not exert too much force on government. In the same ways we use pesticides on fields, politicians are continually trying to damp down opinions in the press that they don't want out there and to promote the opinions that will make their governing easier.

The Fukushima meltdown provides one example of how this happens. It has come out that the British establishment was trying to make sure Fukushima didn't undermine the government's longstanding support for nuclear energy. But it is little surprise that the accident did undermine popular support for nuclear energy. If enough people don't want it then as a political project it's very difficult to pull off. So we need to manipulate and manage public opinion because nuclear technology is an expensive and long-term commitment, and we can't have the fickle public shutting it down at a whim. Such behavior expresses a quite different account of what politics actually is. I mean, there's a whole history, starting with Machiavelli, of understanding the task of governing as essentially one of responding to what fortune throws at you. Politicians today combine that belief with the modern technological impulse to find methods and tools that promise to ensure that we can control all the basic building blocks it takes to keep our societies running.

Once again this chain of reasoning is resonant with the language of *oeconomia*. Politicians understand that modern nations need to keep their economies running well in order not to slip down in the quagmire of powerlessness. So we need to feed our people. But the concern of rulers with the flow of goods and ensuring that the citizenry can eat takes us back to some very old theological themes that remain at play even in a political culture that now approaches these questions under the sway of the idea that these things can not only be fostered and overseen, but can and must be actively controlled, made subservient to political governance. And then the surprise comes, and I think the fall of the Murdoch empire in Britain is a little window into the fact that there is a lot of violence intertwined with that way of doing politics. Murdoch had political power because he controlled opinions. And he could keep the populace on-side or he could turn the populace against a politician.

But now that his unscrupulous deployment of that reach is emerging during the parliamentary hearings that are going on,[3] a frenzy of repressed feeling is exploding among the citizenry, which is realizing they have been manipulated for decades. The surface occasion for this inquest is the actions of a few newspaper editors and reporters involved in telephone hacking. But the hearings are also bringing into view the much larger reality that modern politics, wedded as it is to the press and the spin doctor, function to produce rather than to seek out a political consensus that can be found by seeking that as-yet hidden and therefore surprising common agreement about political decisions that need again and again to be searched out. Once again, now in a political register, there emerges this complex of interlocking refusals to take seriously what is given and we cannot produce.

I would like to build on your observations, taking them in a slightly different direction. You've presented your role as a Christian facilitator as one that brings a different starting point to bear in secular cultural contexts. Could you comment in the first instance on how you bring this challenge to your secular university students, and then how you would challenge them in turn to raise this theologically informed alternative perspective within the larger secular context?

Your language of facilitator appeals to me, and I often also use the similar language of midwifery, because for me one of the icons of the struggle that I've been trying to sketch is the knowledge of the midwife in its contrast with the knowledge of the doctor. The midwife knows all the little tricks of how to get the baby there safely. She has to know how to work with given bodies in their given state and with their given powers, and also that if there is going to need to be any cutting or killing involved, she will have to hand the job over to the doctor. Her knowledge comes through hands-on experience and sometimes involves counter-intuitive therapies such as the application of a warm coffee compress at the right time and in the right place in order to loosen up the fibers of the body in preparation for birth. You could count on someone trained in this knowledge intuitively to understand how to approach the problem of caring in relatively simple ways for an ulcer-ridden chemo patient's mouth.

3. Rupert Murdoch was called before a UK parliamentary committee in (July 2011) that was investigating phone hacking at one of his newspapers and uncovered linkages between his media empire and his role as a political kingmaker.

This is by no means to deny the importance of the doctor, because you may need one sometimes to come in and get the baby out as quickly as possible, using the violence necessary for such surgeries, which we should never forget are really very violent. But this should be the violence of last resort, and it is just as important to be able to deploy it well as it is to see it as genuinely a last resort, and to be used very sparingly because it is not really geared for the normal situation. Incidentally, this would be one of the main reasons why I can imagine Christians being policemen and soldiers, because they should be the ones who have learned from the tradition of just war what it means to deploy violence only as a very last resort. In both human political life and in our care for human bodies, if the modalities of violence become the normal modalities and we lose the sense that the normal modalities should take the given seriously in its integrity, then we are in very big trouble indeed.

It seems to me, unfortunately, that we've lost this understanding of the relation between the normal and the extraordinary. Within the rationality of secular thought, at least since the high Enlightenment split between theoretical and practical knowledge, the doctor is taken to have real knowledge, defined as theoretical and scientifically verified, while the midwife is taken to be only the holder of low-level anecdotal knowledge, that is, practical wisdom. Such practical wisdom is assumed to contribute little of substance to the progress of society. I want to turn this framing of the matter around and say that the emergency nature of highly interventionist violent action, up to and including military action, can't possibly be baseline activity, and if you make it a baseline activity you have no option but to destroy more than your society is creating. The sheer existence of human society rests on more basic and extended forms of fecundity that characterize life. So that's the larger picture.

As an educator I think it is possible to give students a feel for what it means to work like a midwife, give them a tangible sense of what it means to foster such capacities and to explicate them as forms of following Christ. This differs from the church, which says, "We know God and we have a deposit of revelation we are bound to protect, and this revelation and the doctrines associated with it allow us to pronounce on reality beyond what the rest of you can see." This is often played out among evangelicals when they open discussions with non-believing academics by saying, "You can't ground your own thought systems without a theological starting point, and we provide that." There's a power play involved in that gesture. I would rather say that a real facilitator displays what it means that Christianity starts from where people are, listens to their concerns, responding to their perplexities, and tries to build consensus politically; it tries to provoke different ways of paying attention to the social and material worlds that already exist.

It is a temptation to want always to make a decisive intervention in a discussion or to come in and totally alter and remake the landscape of people's perceptions. I don't want to produce students who think that's what they're about either. Without naming any names, we should notice that there are divinity schools that produce students who are very often perceived as zealots of one sort or another. Even though in popular rhetoric it is the evangelicals and fundamentalists who are zealots, I think that modernity is by definition a zealotry. Any Christianity that can say, "Let's look at what is already given to us and what is being given and what we don't receive as given," is a real anti-zealotry alternative. Here I mean zealotry in the sense of the ideologue, rather than in the proper Christian sense of having a passion for God. I try to make this distinction tangible in the context of the classroom by trying to show students why they need not enter discussions with the aim of winning the argument or making the decisive intervention or "refuting the infidel." Such impulses I would take to be yet another expression by Christians of techniques of force that drive the imagination of the modern world. My basic interest is in trying to teach students what it means, in practical terms, to live as if the Lord is faithful in giving the world what it needs. And my job is to direct attention to what God has promised to be up to and to help Christians to follow this lead rather than thinking it's all up to them.

"Modernity as zealotry" is such a concise encapsulation of the issues you have so clearly articulated. Might the whole notion of civil conduct be a product of a Christian theological viewpoint? This seems to be your answer to the situation of dialogical confrontation, where the "rubber meets the road," inasmuch as you are proposing that as a Christian facilitator you are there both to model and mentor a generation in an understanding that is a counterpoint to this modern zealotry.

If I understand your question correctly, I'd say that my position as a sort of public intellectual, if we want to put it that way, is to support one of two trajectories.

We must speak in the face of the zealotry of modernity. This zealotry tends to stand up and in a bald-faced way accuse Christians like myself of being anachronistic holdovers from the age of mystification, vestigial organs of a thought world that is very much on its way out. And in the face of that sort of zealotry the task is just to try to make it as obvious as you can the sense in which a proper full-blown confessing believer belongs at the table. If people are willing to grant that a theologian is at least interesting to have around then I feel free to discuss all the material questions that we've been discussing in such detail in these interviews.

This secular willingness to hear Christians out allows us to say, "Look, on any given topic there are different ways to construe where the problem lies." Modern secularists, simply because secular reason is the dominant framework of meaning in the developed world, won't have at their finger-tips all the alternative ways of approaching an issue that a theologian will. In a sense we're always useful to the academy simply because we have a deeper knowledge of the historical variability of ways of seeing most issues. It behooves Christian theologians to always be able to bring that historical knowledge out at the appropriate time. This theological backdrop allows us to develop sharp discriminations and priorities related to what we believe God is up to in sustaining human life, which also allows the theologian the feeling of being more sure-footed going into specific public discussions. This sense of security allows us to say, "If we take A, B, and C as the core constituents of the problem we are discussing, why don't we think about a different approach to one of those constituents for this or that reason."

Let's return to mobility. We have a transport mobility sub-unit at the University of Aberdeen. And if they have come to some consensus that what we should be after is producing more sustainable ways of organizing our transport infrastructures, then that consensus is based on nothing more than a largely inarticulate moral consensus in some sectors of society. And if I ask them, "Why should we care about that?," they wouldn't necessarily be able to articulate an answer other than to say that it is self-evidently a good thing. You can sometimes press questions about the relation of various priorities as well. If, for instance, people in the transport unit say their main aim is to reduce energy use in transport, sometimes their aims can be set within the larger web of human relations that they effect. Sometimes you need to ask, "Aren't there other moral considerations that are quite important, like accessibility of transport to older people or people with lower mobility. Where does that fit in with how we think about transport?" You can bring in hidden moral considerations, or you can just go along with the moral considerations that seem to be driving the more interesting sub-sections of a discussion. There is a whole range of practical ways you can intervene in an ongoing discussion. It's always wonderful to find someone with whom you can make an alliance and I typically think that's not so difficult in discussions of practical questions.

You've introduced a positive note into what has been a very interesting and constructive critique, having moved on to demonstrate how this critique of modernity actually allows the Christian facilitator to aid the secular culture in reexamining what would otherwise be a rather narrow range of options. You've thereby positioned the Christian facilitator as a constructive agent rather than someone who must argue that Christian community needs to step away from secular culture and create an alternative.

The artificiality of all Christian attempts to isolate themselves from non-Christians is revealed by its impossibility. This is not to suggest that the church and world are indistinguishable. It's entirely legitimate to maintain boundaries of various sorts, though where these boundaries lie and how they are constructed will always require ongoing negotiation—and rightly so. Given that I live six feet from a busy thoroughfare, it is appropriate that my house has granite walls and drapes over the windows, though not because my family is an enclave that is keeping its distance from the public. It's very much a way of being in the public to say that at this point a certain amount of privacy is constitutive of what it means to be a family.

This is why I think the rhetoric that is pretty popular at the moment among conservative Christians about the church being a contrast society is misguided on at least two fronts. First, it's misguided at the level of its assessment of how different the church actually is from the world. Sociologically speaking, especially on environmental issues, it probably isn't even distinguishable in relation to popular trends. That's bound to be true on all sorts of issues, though I hope it's not true on every issue, and I sincerely hope that the church is in the vanguard of living as a group in better and more reconciling ways.

The second problem the contrast model of the church presents arises from its sense that the only thing Christians have to bring to the world is to show it how much it lacks. While the world does lack something in not knowing its heritage or its Creator, I'm not sure that lack of knowledge can be cashed out in the claim that unbelievers don't know anything about the goodness of creation. The only thing the church knows that the world does not is who sustains it. But if it knows this biblically it also knows that the one Lord sustains everyone—the rain falls on the just and the unjust. So the fact that the church knows where the rain comes from or healing comes from or political consensus comes from doesn't mean that it can lord it over everyone else. It ought to inhabit that knowledge through service to everyone else by displaying an uncanny capacity to point them to the things that really sustain them.

We're approaching again from yet another angle the point I have made before about the three estates: the *oeconomia*, the *politia*, and the *ecclesia*. In the *ecclesia* we are taught how God sustains everyone. That God sustains everyone is precisely the reason we can't take up the stance of lording it over others, feeling superior for knowing that it's God sustaining them, even though they don't know that, or at least they don't know it explicitly. They may well know that they are sustained by the natural world and be paying very close attention to processes by which this happens, which even suggests that they may know more of God's grace in certain areas than believers have yet imagined. This, I believe, is another powerful implication of the doctrine of the estates, at least as Luther used it, because it allows us to affirm that non-Christians genuinely know something of God's active grace. If they are good doctors, or parents or teachers, in the sense I have portrayed, not extracting by violence but really receiving and fostering what is given, then they know how to receive what God gives, and in many cases, to our shame, they know this better than Christians.

I think it's sociologically the case that Christians frequently believe that we receive God's care in culturally more sensitive ways than everybody else in society, despite the fact that we go to the same supermarkets, drive the same SUVs, etc. If you're saying the church and the world are different because the church knows how to receive God's care in a way that has become embedded in the institutions we form and the techniques we deploy to achieve what we consider success, I think that's just not accurate, because as we've discussed we're just as likely to take our standards of success from the worst aspects of worldly wisdom. If the church knows who cares for it, then it also knows that God is not only caring for everyone else, but cares for them whether or not they believe. The church is, in my understanding, nothing but the servant of the whole world.

8

Theology in the University, Manicheans Today, Realist Christianity

Please develop any question you would like to address that falls into the overarching question of this series of interviews: "What do you identify as the challenges and most critical issues when presenting environmental ethics in a Christian higher education context?"

I guess I have to say immediately that I don't have much experience working in a Christian higher education context if my secular university is not considered one of those, and that at the same time I don't consider myself a secular academic, in that sense. I consider myself an educator of the church that for historical reasons has ended up educating its ministers at a university where it has the advantage of opening the door to anyone who wants to study theology. I value my context, but in that sense I can't answer the question about the Christian higher education context. In another sense I think wherever a Christian theologian does their ecclesial job she is making her place of work a Christian higher education context.

That was a useful differentiation to begin with. But yes, actually I'm particularly interested in the role of the School of Divinity within a secular university, which differs in important ways from the institutional

arrangements in place in North American culture, and I would think that raises both challenges and opportunities the American counterpart may not offer. What are the challenges you face within a School of Divinity within a larger secular university? What are the direct or indirect critiques, opposition, or opportunities that arise?

Well, currently we are valued pretty highly by the university on familiar neo-liberal grounds, which run, "We're not interested in the material content that you're teaching, but we're interested in the academic standard of your operation, which other academics in the field seem to think is pretty high, which means you must be offering a high quality education." Aberdeen has fared very well in the UK-wide assessment of higher education that happens every five to seven years since it was instituted by Thatcher, which has been called the RAE (Research Assessment Exercise) and is now called the REF (Research Excellence Framework). In the last round (2008), depending on how you calculate the results, we were either in a tie for first place or came a very close second out of all the theological departments in the UK. That's the main interest of university administrators, because the percentages of government funding that go to each university are directly tied to these results. In addition we also attract a good number of students and quite a few post-grads as well, all of whom pay tuition, and many pay a higher rate of overseas tuition. So the bean-counters like us. Odd as it may sound, we're taken to be golden children, formally speaking, compared to other departments in the university because we bring in a lot of money and don't need a lot of expensive equipment. It's a no-brainer really.

But precisely because this is the ruling logic, the position is a dangerous one. There's been some good writing over the last few years asking whether there is anything "unifying" the university any more. It's an institution that is in many cases unified only by the sheer imperative of institutional survival, and can no longer articulate how it remains a collective quest for knowledge that joins up, which has any unity. When the language with which the university was originally described drifted free of its origins in a high medieval Christian cosmology it was bound eventually to become a technical enterprise in which all that can possibly be taken seriously are technical criteria. By technical criteria and financial criteria we're doing really well. Who wants to kill the golden goose? But in an ancient university like ours it always remains possible to speak from that position to draw out vestiges of the original unity out of which the university sprang, not least as marked by our university's motto, "*initium sapientiae timor domini*"—"the fear of the Lord is the beginning of wisdom."

That said, a lecturer in religious studies put together a series called "Soapbox" where he called for people to give polemical papers in a cross-disciplinary faculty context. It was a lovely experience, and funnily enough, at least half of the papers had something to do with religion. There still seems to be a sense in which the only place you can really get an argument going in the university is on the topic of religion because the topic still flushes out quite polarized views. I gave a talk called "Why the University of Aberdeen Needs a Divinity Department," in which I explained why it matters that in Aberdeen we still use the older language of "divinity" rather than the newer more generic langue of a religious studies department.

Could we ask you to explore some highlights of that?

My basic argument was that religious studies, for historical reasons starting in about the 1960s, has conformed to the rationale of the rest of the university, which is that what we are doing is studying things dispassionately. Detached observation as a method can be applied to something called "religion." The label "divinity" says instead, "That's not what we're doing. We're working out of a knowledge base that is premised on existential and conceptual commitment. An investigation in this knowledge base can't proceed in abstraction from our existential commitments." This starting point makes it a different sort of discipline. Put in conceptual terms, religious studies understands itself, like every other social science, to be taking a view that is outside looking in. This also means that it can never be an engine of fresh Christian thinking, because it has set as its task to describe what "those" believers think or have thought. In my view theology must always be a conceptual engine actually producing fresh insight for the church and the world. This suggests that there is an inevitable intellectual stagnation in the shift from theology to religious studies, and that is detrimental to the university because what the university needs from divinity is insight into how the world might be otherwise.

What a brilliant starting point for engagement with secular colleagues.

Thank you, but there were a few academics in the audience who begged to differ. To some of the protests I had to respond, "Just because it starts with belief doesn't mean it's not a genuine discipline with its own terminology and concepts." They know enough about how knowledge works to understand my point that you can't go into the physics lab and say "this is stupid" without understanding it. You can't just say "theology's all hogwash" without doing the donkey work to figure out how the terms function. So I fielded questions along those lines, but a really good academic knows both that this is a true point and not a very important one. The harder and more hostile question came from a lawyer who just said, "It looks to me that divinity is just a vestigial organ." He and I went back and forth and afterward my eminent former colleague John Webster stood up and said, "Well, we've been doing this long before there was a university and we will be doing it long after it has fragmented, so if you don't want us here, that's an arrangement that can be organized." So, in other words . . . the defense of why a school of divinity is in the university can be played at several different levels, and John sort of flagged up the level at which it mattered to the administrators, which is, "You're pretty happy to have us when we're bringing in money." You let the vestigial appendage that you believe at the theoretical level to be hogwash, a pseudo-science, remain in the university because you're greedy, basically. The comment has teeth because it so incisively names the configuration of people's actual commitment to the university.

This raises the question, "What are you here for?" and I think that's a question that theology is very good at asking, "What, really, are we doing here?" Theology doesn't claim to be here for its own self-interest. And in fact, because it's suspicious of its own self-interest, it is able to ask much sharper questions about whether the rest of the disciplines are just here out of self-interest. It's more prestigious to be a professor of sociology when the sociology department still exists, and there are self-interested reasons, therefore, to argue that it should exist. So you can keep a department around for a whole range of reasons, but I argued that the function of divinity is to say "Who is this for?," "Who does it serve?" That's the same question I ended with in our discussion of your fourth question.[1] We need to be asking, "Who does banking serve?" "Who does the manufacturer of sports clothing serve?" Such questions usually get submerged in the hurly-burly of financial considerations and prestige considerations and simply drawing a paycheck. So I position the role of a divinity department in a secular university as, in every concrete sphere, to keep pressing the question,

1. See chapter 6.

"How does our self-interest get in the way of actually serving people, and what does it materially mean to be of service to humanity in whatever field we're working?" A significant decidedly secular minority found that a very provocative and helpful challenge. I also received subsequent invitations to extend the discussion by presenting similar arguments in a string of conferences devoted to thinking more clearly about how we might define the categories of religion and secularity.

The recent crisis in Norway has provided food for thought inasmuch as one of the most successful socialist countries in Western Europe converged around Oslo Cathedral, which was not only an expression of attachment to place but an immersion as a nation in a full-blown liturgical service with not one but three sermons predicated on the work and person of Christ. This service was seen as having a crucial role to play in setting the tone for the recovery of the nation, and culminated last night with 250,000 people, out of a city of 600,000, meeting to affirm that they will not allow their culture to be dominated by hatred but rather to be determined by what they called "love" and "democracy," which they see as encapsulated in the service in the cathedral. [2] **The cathedral is now literally surrounded by a sea of flowers and the people have chosen to make the cathedral the focus of their healing as a nation. That's a provocative image.**

That witness is doubly thought-provoking because the person who committed the atrocity that the nation was mourning also defended his actions as Christian service. Behring Breivik's testament, the "2083 Manifesto," makes it clear that he considers himself to be carrying on the heritage of the crusades from the very first page on which he put the Crusader's Cross. In terms of content the document is made up of all sorts of bits and pieces drawn from American neo- or ultra-conservative material, including big chunks out of the Unabomber Ted Kaczynski 's manifesto. Breivik explicitly says that the clash between Christianity and Islam has gone on for centuries, and locates his murderous actions within the narrative of that larger struggle. The reality of rival Christianities is exposed by this event in Norway, an internal rivalry that is not confined to Norway, I would suggest. The Norwegian assassin sought alliances with various right-wing European

2. This is a reference to the memorial service for those slain by Anders Breivik held in Oslo Cathedral on 30 July 2011.

groups and felt a strong affinity for the US Tea Party movement, which has been so important in shaping the Republican party in the last decade or so, not least because of strong support among evangelical Christians. It's important to at least ask what the common denominator might be.

Richard Hofstadter's classic *The Paranoid Style in American Politics* draws attention to the role of apocalypticism that we discussed earlier.[3] There's a difference between saying that the Russians present a strategic threat to our interests in some form, and saying that if we don't defeat the Russians it will be the end of our civilization and we must immediately do everything we can to destroy them. Hofstadter tries to map how you can start from the same premise, that there is a threat, but how this real-world situation can be interpreted in what he calls a paranoid style: "there is good and evil and the evil is encroaching in all kinds of backdoor hidden ways and it needs to be destroyed root and branch, and it needs to be done now or never, or we're all going to be submerged." That's what theologians have called a Manichean vantage point.

In normal politics you assume when things aren't as you would like that you need to get organized and try to figure out concrete arguments and put your position forward and advance it through political means. That's why the connection with Kaczynski is interesting because Breivik just substituted "cultural Marxists" and "Muslims" for Kazinski's "liberals" and "blacks." There's clearly a convergence of a feeling of marginalization and threat combined with nostalgia for an idealized previous era when men were men and women were women and Americans were Americans, or Norwegians were good Christian Norwegians. An apocalyptic battle is therefore staged in the mind that's an all-or-nothing affair. It's not hard to see that this is not too far from much of the political rhetoric that has been attractive to conservative American Christians for several decades now, who therefore also seemed ready to go to war against "evil empires."

This is why, especially in a North American evangelical context, it's important to be sensitive to the difference between the logic of the arriving eschatological kingdom of peace, which was brought to life by someone who refused to fight to make sure his movement was not squashed—and the ways that story can be inverted into a Christianity which allows us to go to war to protect our clan.

This dynamic also has relevance for the ecological discussion. Some of the more outspoken Christian activists on environmental issues also strike

3. Hofstadter, *The Paranoid Style*, 29–40. See chapter 6.

apocalyptic notes that emphasize that we're fast approaching the point of no return. I think every careful observer of the debates in environmental science would have to at least entertain the thought that we're already past the point of no return and are in for a very rough ride. A sober assessment that takes this observation seriously and sees the magnitude of the problem of turning the ship around in the developed and developing nations is quite different from the other tone of voice that calls for sacrifices and is prepared to vilify people who don't take the same position. For reasons we've already talked about, I'm as worried about that as a political and rhetorical stance as I am about the environmental problem itself.

Could you comment on the theological position that holds that this is all part of God's plan, that there is a divine drama happening in which these are all necessary events pushing us towards a cataclysmic precipice that will conclude with the second coming? The second coming of Christ is rarely discussed outside of the very dramatic writing and film series that have been produced by those who are adherents of the position that this will happen imminently. They would therefore concur that these are critical issues and we may have passed the point of no return and are in for a rough ride, but that is exactly what Scripture says would occur. Could you comment on that thinking?

Biographically, I've spent a lot of time in that cultural universe. But my main interest in the horizon of eternity is not only understanding it as coming in the future, but in thinking about eternity as a different tenor to the current world. That time can be grasped and becomes impregnated with the eternal is clearly signaled in the New Testament by the use of two different Greek terms for time, *chronos* and *kairos*. *Chronos* is normal clock time. *Kairos* is a type of heightening of time that happens in the presence of God. A translation of one of the classic descriptions of the kingdom that Jesus inaugurates is that it is "the fullness of time." The fullness of time is not later, but now. That is why I think, again, that the millennial understanding of history as a sequence of immanent historical events that happen in a linear progression and can be anticipated beforehand because we have a Scriptural blueprint about the second coming is an expression of a deist understanding of God. God is the one who has given us the checklist that allows us to tick off events and know where we are in the countdown.

A couple of weeks ago (21 May 2011) Harold Camping predicted the world would end. His whole calculative operation is not anti-empirical or anti-biblical. It's just deploying a form of reasoning that is not theological enough, on my reading, because it misunderstands time. It thinks of time as essentially linear, unitary, something on spools being unwound on one end and rolled up on the other. This sort of view does all sorts of things to how one reads the Bible. For one thing it cannot admit the ways that the books of Genesis and Revelation function as pieces of literature, nor how Israel or the church understood the intermediate time, the time between the beginning and the end.

The church's genuine present, I really believe, is the communion of saints, and that communion is eternal. Augustine was onto something when he articulated the standard early Christian view that the City of God is comprised of the angels and the dead saints and the living saints. The very idea of "presence" is in this view relational. What is real is who we are with, face to face, which means that the real present is comprised of a communal life in which we living Christians represent only a small portion of the whole. Heavenly time, which is timeless from an earthly perspective, is the real time, but that time touches down in moments of fullness in our clock time world, unveils regular clock time as essentially a deficient version of what time really is.

None of this is meant to suggest that I would deny that some sort of drastic environmental shift could be on its way, such as a shift in the jet stream or ocean currents that markedly alters the weather and climate patterns on which our civilizations have been built. Such changes would produce real human suffering on a grand scale. This would have a type of "end times" galvanizing effect on the world population, and I can imagine this being God's way of helping us to get together and be more responsible on environmental issues. But I would not want to assume that this means that the second coming is closer now than it was yesterday, because like most Christians through the ages, I believe Jesus when he said that he could be returning this very hour, and warned us off the game of trying to predict his arrival.

Stephen Hawking says that he has come to the conclusion that for string theory to work there must be parallel universes, at least seven by his reckoning. Someone asked him, very provocatively, "On that basis, do you believe that these parallel universes have any points of convergence?" And

he hypothesized there was certainly some correlations between them. At which point someone said, "Does that explain the presence of angels or heaven or hell? Are we in fact scientifically approaching something that was more simplistically identified by way of revelation in another era?" And he paused and said, "Well, I'm not sure I can speak about heaven, but it certainly opens up the possibility of purgatory."

Now, I thought that was a very interesting comment because as a scientist he is a man who has divorced his Christian spouse who had stood by him for years and has now remarried. Nevertheless, purely on the basis of his own studies he had to concede for the first time in a university context that he could see the legitimacy of a theological vocabulary and conceptual framework because of its resonances with what he was now pursuing in the area of quantum physics.

I found that to be quite intriguing. And of course we have Michael Polanyi's famous hypothesis that if all objects determine the criteria by which they will be known, then should God exist, that God, too, as an actual entity, would determine the criteria by which God would be known, which opens up a philosophical and mathematical basis for divine revelation.

I like how you've portrayed Hawking as feeling forced, driven, one might even say "taken captive" by what he observes about the material universe, filtered through mathematics, to truth claims that he finds uncomfortable and just has to deal with. At the same time I'm uncomfortable with "gotcha" apologetic strategies that are always looking for ways to show unbelievers why a "Christian worldview" is more coherent or already knows what others have just discovered. I prefer the apologetics of having Christians' action matching their speech. One way this can happen is when Christians, in being "taken captive" by Christ, live as those who have been freed to very readily and humbly admit that creation is more complex than we have yet imagined. You might say that because they have repented before the Creator, Christians should be more ready to give up the illusions and misunderstandings they know they hold about other creatures and so be quicker and suppler learners. Knowing the world well is really a spiritual stance and I'm interested in empowering Christians and through them the world to see and learn to accommodate themselves with attentive care to reality as it is.

I read a great line the other day from the historian L. B. Namier, who said that "the crowning attainment of historical study" is to achieve "an intuitive sense of how things do not happen."[4] I think that's right. Historical study as a discipline with its own parameters is important and helpful in asking certain sorts of questions and forming certain sort of judgments. I worked for a little while as a newspaper reporter and an editorialist as well. To be a reporter you have to learn how to "read" brute reality, like the historian, but with slightly different lenses. But the point is that you have to learn. There are certain "facts" in front of you, but the story is a construct resting on a whole range of bits and pieces of narrative and people's observations that are at your disposal but don't yield one coherent narrative unity. Journalism is the art of producing a certain type of fluid and solid narrative out of these bits, which is why there are better and worse journalists. Finding the narrative that holds all the pieces pretty firmly together is a skill-set not entirely different from the lawyer's or detective's. It grows from a desire to, and a skill of, understanding what can and can't happen in both registers—the historical and the journalistic. It's powerful, but it's powerful because it's limited in specific ways.

I felt those limits quite acutely as a newspaper journalist and editorialist. In a newspaper editorial you can basically argue for or against things that have been proposed or are in the public eye: for or against nuclear power, for or against Sky TV being bought by the Murdochs. But you rarely have the time or the logical apparatus in place to challenge in deep ways the terms of the debate. One effect of our public discourse being carried out in a forum like the press is that it generates conceptual either-or's that are politically frustrating or which overly constrain what it means to be politically involved. In this forum the illusion is created that if you're going to get involved in an environmental issue you have to be for carbon taxes or against carbon taxes. This sets up a list of very narrowly constrained problem questions that are available in the public discourse, and you're either for or against them.

As I've been presenting it, I think theology is at its best when it is utterly clear that its basic environment is the environment of God's works: sustaining, creating, redeeming. The life of faith is therefore learning to be attentive to God's works in the material world, in this like the empirical scientist, as well as God's activity in the world of events, of history, in this being like the journalist. This is why as an intellectual pursuit, theology is a discourse that allows us to at least change the terms of problems as we have inherited them. But it can do this only if it has served a transformation

4. Namier, "History," 375.

of what we see to be going on, what we see to be present. In my view the biblical writers are our models here. Their narration of what was "really" happening was determined by what they saw God up to, and this produced a reading of events with a narrative unity that non-believers simply could not see, even though all the same "facts" were on view. The New Testament encapsulates this alternative perception in the story of the Emmaus Road encounter (Luke 24:13–35).

We now have a point of entry into your main question with its emphasis on revelation and studying or being responsive to the world as it is. Purely empirical study can question the sort of bald polarities that our public discourse forces on us. Simply being committed to seeing what's actually there in a social situation or in the material world helps to break down or undermine, confound water-tight either/or's. You're either for or against carbon tax, for example. If you look into that question in any detail you see that there are plenty of trade-offs with the carbon-tax system. That doesn't mean we shouldn't participate in this system. But it does mean that the idea that Christians could prove the validity of their Christianity by being for or against carbon tax is a short-circuiting of crucial modes of thinking and acting in viewing environmental issues to be discussed in abstraction from our whole lives and in allowing the discussion of how we might live responsibly to be narrowed to one single, incomplete, policy initiative.

My whole train of thought thus grows from theological sensibilities about the importance of taking seriously historical Christianity's insistence that Christianity is a realist discourse. Theology is concerned with a real God, not a set of symbols that help us live into existential truth or give our lives meaning. It's about a real person, the Trinitarian God, and it's about a creation that existed before us. When we understand theology this way I believe it brings the theologian into alliances with all those human investigations that hold themselves and their descriptions up against the standard of the world as it exists. We can have a serious conversation with a molecular biologist that will be fruitful in our talk about ethics of genetic intervention, but only if everyone is starting from the premise that the creation is out there functioning as given and that we first have to conform our language and thought to it enough to even have a serious discussion about how we should respond to it.

What this also means is theology isn't confined to one idiom or mode of argumentation as is history or journalism. A historian has to speak within a very specific understanding of cause and effect and institutional structure, and observe the genre rules of historical writing. Every newspaper article is constructed in the same way as well, lede first, summary of the basic narrative second, comments and interviews third. But theology doesn't have to adhere to such formulas. We need not write in one idiom, a fact that becomes more obvious if you read around even cursorily in the Christian tradition. By far the nicest piece of theology that I've encountered in the last month is Terrence Malick's feature film *The Tree of Life*, which is not a written text at all. Even for a film it has remarkably little dialogue. And its very refusal to be a script of words in favor of communicating through a sequenced framework of images in order to convey a theological insight I found really quite stimulating. I think theologians ought to think more about how to step outside of the idioms that constrain them in order to point toward the works of a living God.

Bibliography

ORIGINAL INTERVIEWS

For Chapters 1 and 2

Herman Paul and Bart Wallet. "Christelijke ethiek is geen karakterkwestie: Waarom Brian Brock liever psalmen zingt dan hermeneutiekbedrijft," *Wapenveld* 60:5 (October 2010) 12–19. Parts of the interviews were also published in the Dutch Christian newspaper *Nederlands Dagblad* 67.17.537 (October 30, 2010) 18–19. Online: http://www .nd.nl/images/library/PDF/101030.pdf. An edited version of the raw interviews was later published in book form in *Oefenplaatsen: Tegendraadse theologen over kerk en ethiek*, edited by Herman Paul and Bart Wallet, 111–26. Zoetermeer: Uitgeverij Boekencentrum, 2012.

For Chapters 3 through 8

Jacqueline Lee Hall Broen. "The Nagle Brock Interview Series: Higher Education and Environmental Ethics." M. Litt thesis submitted to the University of St. Andrews, 2011.

SELECTED WORKS BY THE AUTHOR

Brock, Brian. "Attunement to Saints Past and Present: Clarifications and Convergences." *European Journal of Theology* 18:2 (2009) 155–64.
———. "Christian Ethics." In *Mapping Modern Theology: A Thematic and Historical Introduction*, edited by Kelly M. Kapic and Bruce L. McCormack, 293–317. Grand Rapids: Baker Academic, 2012.
———. *Christian Ethics in a Technological Age*. Grand Rapids: Eerdmans, 2010.
———. "Creation: Mission as Gardening." In *Living Witness: Explorations in Missional Ethics*, edited by Andy Draycott and Jonathan Rowe, 57–78. Nottingham: Apollos, 2012.
———. "Praise: The Prophetic Public Presence of the Mentally Disabled." In *Blackwell Companion to Christian Ethics*, 2d ed., edited by Stanley Hauerwas and Sam Wells, 139–51. Oxford: Wiley-Blackwell, 2011.
———. *Singing the Ethos of God*. Grand Rapids: Eerdmans, 2007.
Brock, Brian, and Stephanie Brock. "The Disabled in the New World of Genetic Testing: A Snapshot of Shifting Landscapes." In *Theology, Disability and the New Genetics: Why*

Science Needs the Church, edited by John Swinton and Brian Brock, 29–43. London: T. & T. Clark, 2007.

Brock, Brian, Walter Doerfler, and Hans Ulrich. "Genetics, Conversation and Conversion: A Discourse at the Interface of Molecular Biology and Christian Ethics." In *Theology, Disability and the New Genetics: Why Science Needs the Church*, edited by John Swinton and Brian Brock, 146–60. London: T. & T. Clark, 2007.

Brock, Brian, and Bernd Wannenwetsch. "Ein moralisches Angebot für die 'Generation Porno.'" *Saltzkorn* 242 (April/June 2010) 92–97.

Works by Others

Adorno, Theodor. *Minima Moralia: Reflections from a Damaged Life.* Translated by E. F. N. Jephcott. London: Verso, 1978.

Banner, Michael. *Christian Ethics and Contemporary Moral Problems.* Cambridge: Cambridge University Press, 1999.

Barrett, C. K. *The First Epistle to the Corinthians*, 2d ed. London: A. & C. Black, 1971.

Brown, Patricia Leigh. "When the Uprooted Put Down Roots." *New York Times* (9 October 2011). Online: http://www.nytimes.com/2011/10/10/us/refugees-in-united-states-take-up-farming.html?pagewanted=all&_r=0.

Crighton, Ryan. "I'll halt £700m resort plans over turbines, warns Trump." *The Press and Journal* (15 September 2011). Online: http://www.pressandjournal.co.uk/Article.aspx/2437646.

Draycott, Andy. "Preaching: The Free Public Speech of the Prophethood of Believers." In *Living Witness: Explorations in Missional Ethics*, edited by Andy Draycott and Jonathan Rowe, 114–36. Nottingham: Apollos, 2012.

Edwards, Rob. "Revealed: British Government's plan to play down Fukishima." *The Guardian.* (30 June 2011.) Online: http://www.theguardian.com/environment/2011/jun/30/british-government-plan-play-down-fukishima.

Ellul, Jacques. *The Meaning of the City.* Translated by Dennis Pardee. Grand Rapids: Eerdmans, 1993.

Ford, Martin. "Deciding the Fate of a Magical, Wild Place." *Journal of Irish and Scottish Studies* 4:2 (2011) 33–74.

Gorringe, Timothy. Review of *Christian Ethics in a Technological Age*, by Brian Brock. *Conversations in Religion and Theology* 9:1 (May 2011) 35–47.

Gunton, Colin E. *The Barth Lectures.* Edited by P. H. Brazier. London: T. & T. Clark, 2007.

Halberstam, David. *The Powers that Be.* New York: Knopf, 1979.

Hauerwas, Stanley. "Abortion, Theologically Understood." In *The Hauerwas Reader*, edited by John Berkman and Michael Cartwright, 603–22. Durham, NC: Duke University Press, 2001.

Hofstadter, Richard. *The Paranoid Style in American Politics and Other Essays.* New York: Vintage, 2008.

Hunter, James. *To Change the World: The Irony, Tragedy and Possibility of Christianity in the Late Modern World.* Oxford: Oxford University Press, 2010.

Illich, Ivan. *Celebration of Awareness: A Call for Institutional Revolution.* Harmondsworth: Penguin, 1970.

James, P. D. *The Children of Men*. London: Faber and Faber, 1992.

Jennings, Willie James. *The Christian Imagination: Theology and the Origins of Race*. New Haven, CT: Yale University Press, 2010.

Jonas, Hans. *The Imperative of Responsibility: In Search of an Ethics for the Technological Age*. Chicago: University of Chicago Press, 1984.

Kant, Immanuel. *Critique of Pure Reason*. Translated and edited by Paul Guyer and Allen W. Wood. Cambridge: Cambridge University Press, 1997.

Kimmelman, Michael. "In a Bronx Complex, Doing Good Mixes with Looking Good." *New York Times* (26 September 2011). Online: http://www.nytimes.com/2011/09/26/arts/design/via-verde-in-south-bronx-rewrites-low-income-housing-rules.html?pagewanted=all.

Luther, Martin. "The Large Catechism." In *The Book of Concord: The Confessions of the Evangelical Lutheran Church*, edited by Robert Kolb and Timothy J. Wengert, translated by Charles Arand et al., 377–480. Minneapolis: Fortress, 2000.

———. "The Small Catechism." In *The Book of Concord: The Confessions of the Evangelical Lutheran Church*, edited by Robert Kolb and Timothy J. Wengert, translated by Charles Arand et al., 345–75. Minneapolis: Fortress, 2000.

Namier, L. B. "History and Political Culture." In *The Varieties of History: From Voltaire to the Present*, edited by Fritz Stern, 371–87. New York: Merdian, 1956.

Pollan, Michael. *The Omnivore's Dilemma: A Natural History of Four Meals*. New York: Penguin, 2006.

Prather, Scott. *Christ, Power and Mammon: Karl Barth and John Howard Yoder in Dialogue*. London: Bloomsbury, 2013.

Rawls, John. *A Theory of Justice*. Cambridge, MA: The Belknap Press of Harvard University Press, 1971.

Calum, Ross. "Councillors 'Damaged Public Trust.'" *Aberdeen Press and Journal* (13 October 2010). Online: http://www.pressandjournal.co.uk/Article.aspx/1960850.

Scahill, Jeremy. *Blackwater: The Rise of the World's Most Powerful Mercenary Army*. New York: Nation Books, 2008.

Serres, Michel, with Bruno LaTour. *Conversations on Science, Culture, and Time*. Translated by Roxanne Lapidus. Ann Arbor, MI: University of Michigan Press, 1995.

Spink, Kathryn. *The Miracle, the Message, the Story: Jean Vanier and L'Arche*. London: Darton, Longman & Todd, 2006.

Stringfellow, William. *My People Is the Enemy: An Autobiographical Polemic*. Reprint. Eugene, OR: Wipf & Stock, 2008.

Ulrich, Hans G. "On Finding Our Place: Christian Ethics in God's Reality." *European Journal of Theology* 18:2 (2009) 137–44.

Ward, Bob. "You've Been Trumped: Film Reveals Tycoon's Ruthless Efforts to Build Scottish Golf Resort." *The Guardian* (13 September 2011). Online: http://www.theguardian.com/environment/blog/2011/sep/13/youve-been-trumped-scotland-golf-course.

Wannenwetsch, Bernd. "Conversing with the Saints as they Converse with Scripture: In Conversation with Brian Brock's *Singing the Ethos of God*." *European Journal of Theology* 18:2 (2009) 125–35.

Wenham, Gordon J. "Reflections on *Singing the Ethos of God*." *European Journal of Theology* 18:2 (2009) 115–24.

Wolin, Sheldon S. *Politics and Vision: Continuity and Innovation in Western Political Thought*. Princeton, NJ: Princeton University Press, 2004.

14765620R00099

Made in the USA
San Bernardino, CA
03 September 2014